Handbook

3rd edition | © 2013

SMART Recovery®

7304 Mentor Avenue

Suite F

Mentor OH 44060

Toll free | 866-951-5357

440-951-5357

Fax | 440-951-5358

E-mail | info@smartrecovery.org

www.smartrecovery.org

Published by Alcohol & Drug Abuse Self-Help Network, Inc. dba SMART Recovery®

Rosemary Hardin, editor

(Rev. 1-2014)

Table of Contents

Introduction

You may be reading this Handbook because you're suffering from an addictive behavior or someone you love is. Whatever reason you're here, we welcome you to SMART Recovery.

SMART stands for Self Management And Recovery Training. SMART is a nonprofit organization with a mission to offer free, self-empowering, mutual-help groups for abstaining from any substance or activity addiction.

You're not alone. Many people will struggle with a serious addictive behavior during their life.

Whether you're dealing with addictive or compulsive behaviors or substance abuse, SMART has information, tools, and techniques that may help you replace your self-destructive behaviors with healthier options.

People with drinking and substance-abuse addictive behaviors — including smoking — and behavioral issues, such as compulsive gambling or sexual activity, self-harm, and eating disorders, find that SMART provides the support and tools that help them recover.

Recovery is difficult, but with persistence, effort, and support, you can take back your life.

Experience shows that people in recovery are more successful when they receive support from friends, family, and mental health professionals. If you're a concerned significant other — parent, partner, friend, or relative — of someone who abuses substances or engages in compulsive behaviors, this Handbook may help you understand your loved one's issues. SMART also has a Family & Friends Handbook that's available from our online bookstore. If you're a teenager, the Teen Handbook is for you.

This Handbook is written in simple, straightforward language. While it's written with the recovering person in mind, it's also a valuable resource for anyone touched by or interested in addictive behaviors.

There are few absolutes in recovery. What works for one person in one situation may not work for another in the same situation. With that in mind, we avoid words like "must" and "should" and instead present ideas that have helped many of our participants.

SMART is a science-based program. It's built upon well-established scientific approaches used to help people manage behavioral problems and achieve successful change. When new information becomes available, SMART Recovery adjusts its program. There's a more in-depth discussion of the science behind SMART in chapter 7.

In this Handbook, you'll find:

- SMART's 4-Point Program®

- Tools, strategies, and exercises to help you in your recovery

- Information for family and friends

- The science behind SMART
- Reading, websites, and other resources

The SMART community

We offer face-to-face meetings in many countries including the United States, Australia, United Kingdom, and Canada. Volunteers translated our 2nd edition Handbook into Spanish, German, Portuguese, Farsi, Mandarin Chinese, and Danish. We hope to have this edition translated by volunteers, too.

Our online meetings reach a global community. Our meetings — face-to-face and online — are for people in recovery, but there are Family & Friends meetings, too. Anyone may attend any of our meetings except for those listed as "closed."

We aren't a membership-based organization so there's nothing to join. Trained volunteers facilitate all of our meetings and serve in many other roles. They generously share their experience, knowledge, and compassion, and are the backbone of the SMART community.

By buying this Handbook, you support our work of:

- Providing free face-to-face and online mutual-help meetings.
- Providing forums for learning about and discussing addictive behaviors.
- Advocating for choice in help for addictive behaviors.

Acknowledgements

Special thanks to the people who generously gave their time and expertise to create this version of the SMART Handbook: Dr. William Abbott, Jim Braastad, John Frahm, Rosemary Hardin, Randy Lindel, and Richard Phillips.

A very special thank you to Henry Steinberger, the author and editor of SMART's 2nd edition Handbook, which is the foundation for this version.

Disclaimer

Our program isn't intended to be a substitute for professional help or treatment. While SMART does help many people who work toward recovery on their own, it's also a useful supplement to professional help. If you have serious difficulties with alcohol, drugs, compulsive gambling or sexual behaviors, overeating, self-harm, or other dangerous problems, we recognize that you may benefit from professional help in addition to working the SMART program.

To find a mental health professional in your area who subscribes to SMART's principles, visit www.smartrecovery.org.

OK, let's get started . . .

Chapter 1: **Welcome to SMART**

What is SMART?

SMART Recovery started in 1994. SMART, an acronym for Self-Management and Recovery Training, emphasizes "self" — your role in your recovery. We're a nonprofit, science-based program that helps people recover from addictive behaviors.

Whether your addictive behavior involves substances — alcohol, smoking, or drugs — or behaviors — gambling, sex, eating, shopping, self-harm — SMART can help. We understand the work ahead of you. No matter what your addictive behavior, you're not alone.

How SMART works

SMART Recovery uses techniques from Cognitive Behavior Therapy (CBT), Rational Emotive Behavior Therapy (REBT), and Motivational Enhancement Therapy (MET, a nonconfrontational approach to helping people change behaviors). Our organization helps you apply these techniques to your recovery, as guided by our 4-Point Program® (page 2).

Here's how SMART works:

1. We help you look at your behaviors so you can decide what problems need your attention. We also help you stay motivated if you make the decision to change.

2. If you feel you need to work with a therapist in your recovery, we encourage you to do that. If this isn't an option because you can't afford it or live in an area where help is not easily accessible, SMART can still help you.

3. We encourage you to attend SMART meetings. Interacting with others in recovery will help you understand you're not alone as you struggle with the challenges of recovery. At the same time, you're helping others. Many of us who have walked the path of recovery have found great strength in the heartfelt words of others overcoming similar issues. If you choose to pursue recovery without attending meetings, we're still here to help.

You can use SMART's tools, strategies, and resources from the start of your journey to long after you reach your recovery goals.

You can stay in SMART as long as you wish. You aren't making a lifetime commitment to the program. Many find that participating in SMART after they recover helps them avoid relapses. Some volunteer to facilitate SMART meetings or lend their talents and skills in other ways. Others simply continue to attend meetings to share their experiences with people new to SMART, like you.

We focus on the present — and what you want for your future — rather than the past. We discourage the use of labels such as "addicts," "alcoholics," "druggies," "overeaters," etc. because we believe they interfere with a healthy self-image. Instead, we focus on behaviors and how to change them.

Addictive behaviors can arise from both substance use (psychoactive substances including alcohol, nicotine, caffeine, food, illicit drugs, and prescribed medications) and activities (gambling, sex, eating, shopping, relationships, exercise, etc.). Most of us experience an addictive behavior to some degree in our lives. Many people have more than one, either at the same time or they overcome one only to find themselves dealing with another one later.

It's important to remember as you begin your journey that there is not a single "right" way to recovery. We all do it a little bit differently.

The 4-Point Program

The 4-Point Program is the heart of SMART. Each point provides you with tools, techniques, and strategies that can help you on your journey. Many of these tools and techniques are skills you can use after you have fully recovered to help you deal with future problems and achieve more satisfaction and balance in your life.

These points are not steps. For some people they are sequential, for others they are not. For example, some people come to SMART when they are coping with urges, having built their motivation on their own.

The four points are:

1 – **Building and Maintaining Motivation**

2 – **Coping with Urges**

3 – **Managing Thoughts, Feelings, and Behaviors**

4 – **Living a Balanced Life**

Rational Emotive Behavior Therapy

REBT, generally recognized as the first form of Cognitive Behavior Therapy (CBT), was pioneered by Dr. Albert Ellis in the 1950s and was originally known as Rational Therapy.

Many of the tools and techniques that SMART uses come from CBT.

Epictetus, an ancient Greek philosopher, wrote, "People are disturbed not by things but by their view of things."

People sometimes exaggerate their thoughts about events in their lives. These thinking errors, in turn, influence how they feel. This connection forms the underlying principle of REBT:

- **Rational** – How we *think,* which influences . . .
- **Emotive** – How we *feel*, which influences . . .
- **Behavior** – How we *act.*
- **Therapy** – The training to help us learn how to change our thinking to feel and behave in healthier ways.

Many of our problems seem to start with how we react to life's events. If someone is rude to us, we fight with our spouse, or we don't get the job we wanted, our irrational thoughts and excessive emotions may take over.

You may have used an addictive behavior to deal with irrational thoughts and excessive emotions. We call this the "using strategy" for coping with discomfort. Somehow, we adopted the unrealistic belief that life should be free from discomfort and pain, and that we shouldn't have to tolerate it. This unhelpful belief leads to further distress, which drives the urge to engage in addictive behavior to escape the discomfort.

There's more about REBT in chapters 4 and 5.

How is SMART different from other recovery programs?

While SMART can help you as a stand-alone program, it also can work as a companion to professional therapy. If you're working with a mental health professional — counselor, psychologist, or psychiatrist — SMART can augment that work by reinforcing common therapeutic principles.

You also may be working other mutual-help programs. While some of the SMART principles may be different from other programs, many people find that working more than one program at the same time benefits their recovery.

We don't take a position on any other program or therapy. Any given therapy or program doesn't help every person. While thousands of people around the world find SMART to be beneficial, some don't find our program to be helpful. Only you can decide what works best for you. We encourage you to find the help that works for you.

Your recovery is what's important, not which program helps you get there.

Can SMART help me?

The only way you'll know for sure is to try.

Our meetings are designed to deal with the pressing needs of participants. Trained facilitators lead all of our meetings. Our facilitators either have gone through recovery or have a strong desire to help those who are in recovery. All meetings have volunteer medical or mental health advisors. They don't attend meetings but are available to help facilitators with difficult meeting issues.

SMART Recovery Online

You can get confidential support and information from the SMART Recovery Online (SROL) community when you can't or don't want to attend a face-to-face meeting, or you just want another way to connect to others in recovery. We have an active and robust online presence. There are meetings, a chat room, and a message board that are monitored by trained volunteers. There also is extensive information about SMART and our tools, and current information for participants, family and friends, teens, and for volunteers and facilitators.

To sign up for SROL, go to our website and click on the "message boards" link on the homepage; follow the instructions.

Message board — After you sign up for SROL, we invite you to introduce yourself in the "Welcome Area" message board. The main parts of the message board are "Discussions" and "Tools and Resources." The "Classic Posts" section is an archive of some favorite posts from the past. Many people join one or more of the daily check-in groups. There also are forums for specific substances and behaviors — opiates, smoking, eating disorders, self-harm, etc. — as well as for specific situations — family and friends, dealing with grief, recovering to parenthood, health care providers, etc.

Chat room — It's open all day, every day. Because there are online participants from all over the world, there is usually always someone in the chat room. Upon entering, you may find the conversation casual and light-hearted, but if you have an issue or want information, let the room know. Recovery comes first and the focus of the discussion will change to help you.

Meeting rooms — These are where our online meetings happen. There are many meetings each day. Check the drop-down menu at the top of every SMART webpage for a meeting schedule. Some of the meetings are text only, and some are in the voice meeting room where you can participate either by talking over your computer's microphone or by typing like you do in text-only meeting rooms and in the chat room. You're welcome to attend any online meeting, and because you're new to SMART, we encourage you to try out one of the meetings geared toward new participants. Each SROL meeting lasts 90 minutes and is hosted by a trained volunteer facilitator.

Online library — This is an excellent place to find SMART's tools, worksheets, strategies, and methods. Many newcomers print and complete the Cost-Benefit Analysis (CBA) worksheet. You also will find links to our podcasts and YouTube videos, and to the SMART Recovery blog, which we continually update with relevant articles and posts.

Basic terms

SMART uses a lot of acronyms and phrases. Here are the most common. For a complete list, see Appendix A.

Abstinence: Stopping all use of a substance such as alcohol or drugs, or a compulsive behavior such as sex or overeating. Obviously, if you compulsively overeat, you can't give up food, but you can define abstinence as not engaging in compulsive overeating. Chapter 2 addresses this in more detail.

Act out: Engaging in the compulsive behavior you want to stop. If you compulsively cut yourself, then you're acting out when you cut into your body with a sharp object. If you spend money compulsively, signing up for a new credit card or spending hours on shopping websites may be how you act out.

Addictive behavior: Any substance use or activity (gambling, sex, spending, etc.) that you are abstaining from, or are considering abstaining from.

Craving: The thought of doing the behavior you're trying to give up.

Lapse: Sometimes called a slip. It's a brief return to old behavior. Someone who's abstained from gambling for several years lapses when she plays an online gambling game or spends an hour — maybe even a weekend — gambling in Vegas.

Relapse: A sustained return to the old behavior. If she goes back to her old gambling behavior by repeatedly playing online games or making trips to the nearest casino, that's a relapse.

Trigger: Any cue — a smell, image, event, sound, time of day, etc. — that triggers an urge, which drives a person to act out. This doesn't mean a trigger automatically leads to acting out; however, many of our irrational thoughts and excessive emotions may be connected to these triggers, especially in the early stages of recovery. Triggers (also called cues) are associations that spark urges. For example:

- Driving past his favorite bar may trigger an urge to drink for someone who has a problem with alcohol. A woman suffering from compulsive sexual behaviors may feel an urge triggered by the smell of a certain brand of aftershave.

Urge: A strong, compelling desire to do the behavior you want to abstain from.

Using: A common term that refers to substance abuse but can apply to any addictive behavior. We use when we engage in any compulsive behavior to escape our discomfort.

Tools, exercises, and strategies

Throughout this Handbook, there are items marked **TOOL**, **EXERCISE**, or **STRATEGY**. These are SMART aides that may be very helpful in your recovery.

Chapter 2: **Getting Started**

'Where do I start?'

When you decide to change your life, especially after years of unhealthy behaviors, it can seem intimidating and overwhelming. We know — most of us involved in writing this Handbook have first-hand experience with recovery.

It may seem like the problems you created for yourself are beyond your ability to fix. One strategy for dealing with such daunting problems is to break them down into smaller pieces, or "chunk" them so that you can deal with one or two parts of an issue at a time.

This Handbook starts by helping you understand some new ideas, which may help reduce some of the fears and anxiety you may have about recovery.

Understanding addictive behaviors

If we engage in a behavior once in a while and don't do it to excess, then we don't need to worry about it, analyze it, or stop it; however, if a behavior — even one that starts out as a healthy one — causes too many problems in our lives, it may be time to change.

Behaviors become addictive when they:

- Are the result of a pattern that becomes a ritual or habitual.
- Become stronger each time you do them.
- Involve short-term thinking in the pursuit of immediate pleasure, to feel "normal," or to relieve discomfort or distress.
- Incur long-term costs, such as damaged relationships or serious financial hardship.

We reinforce and strengthen our addictive behavior when we are caught up in the repeating pattern of giving into urges to get relief (Figure 2.1).

The Problem of Immediate Gratification

A trigger leads to a thought or craving (*I want a drink, some meth, to gamble, to have sex, to eat*), which builds into an urge (*I need a drink, some meth, etc.*). Once we use or do, we feel better or normal, but only for a while. This is the Problem of Immediate Gratification, or PIG.

Figure 2.1. **The PIG's method.**

| Trigger —
An event | Craving —
I want to use | Urge —
I need to use | Act out/use —
I feel better now |

The problem with the PIG is that immediate gratification often has greater influence on us than healthier, delayed rewards. Repeating the pattern reinforces the PIG. Every time we give into an urge, we strengthen the pattern. The next urge comes more quickly and more forcefully. More — and less important — events, thoughts, feelings, and other life stuff cause you discomfort, which triggers more cravings, resulting in more urges, which leads to more using.

The minor stresses that earlier in your life you dismissed as annoying are now major issues in your mind, giving you a "reason" to use. Over time you need more of your addictive behavior to find relief, so you may start looking for or inventing triggers to have an excuse to use. You may even create urges so that you'll have an excuse to act out.

The more you repeat this pattern, the bigger the PIG grows.

You may feel like you can't escape this cycle of addictive behavior and that you're doomed to repeat it forever. But there is hope; millions of people have permanently stopped their compulsive behaviors and moved on to live satisfying lives. It happens every day!

How to defeat an addictive behavior

It all starts with stopping. If you don't give in to urges, they become less intense and occur less frequently. Fewer things will serve as triggers so you'll have fewer urges. The PIG shrinks.

Learning to tolerate short-term discomfort, and accepting that urges won't feel good for seconds to minutes until they fade enables you to control your behavior. Within a relatively short time — a few days or weeks — you'll learn to accept short-term discomfort as part of living a healthier life. Your addictive behavior will lose its grip on your life. You'll understand that using is a choice. Just by understanding that using is a choice and not an inevitable reaction to discomfort, you're already retraining your brain.

Your recovery can be a realistic and self-directed journey; SMART can help you:

- Identify and understand the triggers that lead to your cravings and urges, and that they don't have to result in acting out.

- Recognize and understand your unhealthy patterns (rituals, triggers, and behaviors), and stay motivated and focused, even when recovery seems overwhelming.

- Cope with your urges, change how you think about the events in your life, and make better decisions.

Is addiction a disease or behavior?

This question is debated within the recovery and treatment field. SMART Recovery tools can help you whether or not you believe addiction is a disease.

Understanding recovery

What is recovery? You might think this is an obvious question with a clear answer; however, it really isn't. In fact, it's rather complex.

SAMHSA (Substance Abuse and Mental Health Services) defines recovery as "A process of change through which individuals improve their health and wellness, live a self-directed life, and strive to reach their full potential."

SMART has long recognized recovery as the most important part of success in managing addictive behavior. Many mental health professionals consider recovery as a separate focus in the overall management of addictive behavior. Some current and recent government-supported research in this field focus on recovery. In the United States, events such as Recovery Month, designated as every September, raise awareness about recovery.

Recovery is different for everyone. Yours may be about changing negative thinking patterns. In addition to abstaining from unwanted behaviors, you also may commit to trying new activities that challenge you. You may choose to create more time for your loved ones. Recovery helps you fill the void — once occupied by your addictive behavior — with healthier thoughts, emotions, activities and challenges that lead you to a more balanced and satisfying life.

Abstinence without recovery doesn't provide people with the tools and information they need to fill the addictive behavior void, which is why lapses and relapses are more common than in abstinence with recovery.

Recovery is about learning to replace unhealthy behaviors with healthier activities, leading to a more balanced life. Recovery is a personal journey. It's what you make it and can be how you want it to be. After all, you're the boss!

Unhelpful labels

Perhaps you've been told, "You're an alcoholic"; "You're a drunk"; "You're weak"; "You're different from normal people"; "You will battle this for the rest of your life"; "You must stop right now and forever"; to which you may have responded, "I'll never beat this so I might as well (*act out, get drunk, get stoned, smoke a pack of cigarettes, eat cookies, go shopping, harm myself*) because I can never be healthy. Why bother?"

You may feel trapped in your behavior with little hope. Hopelessness often fuels addictive behavior. This is why SMART discourages the use of labels.

The journey to recovery

Like any long journey, recovery starts with one step. Changing behavior patterns takes time and effort, trial and error.

If you have ever thought, "I'm a hopeless addict with a disease that I will never beat"; "I have no choice but to fight this forever"; or "I have no choice but to keep using"; try changing your thoughts to, "I used to have an addictive behavior but I choose not to act that way any more." Those words may help you feel more confident, especially in the beginning of your recovery.

If you can feel that you will triumph over your unwanted behavior, then it's likely you will. If one of SMART's tools, strategies, or exercises doesn't work for you, try a different one until you find what makes you successful. Recovery is possible. Urges fade away. Abstinence gets easier. Your addictive behavior becomes a thing of your past. You find meaning and enjoyment in your new life.

Abstinence vs. moderation

SMART is an abstinence-based program. The idea of abstinence may be intimidating to you — perhaps even distasteful — as you begin your recovery. Even if you're unsure about abstinence, you're still welcome at our meetings.

For alcohol and drug use, the meaning of abstinence is clear: Stop drinking or using. That also works for some compulsive behaviors, such as gambling, because one doesn't need to gamble to survive.

But what about other activities such as eating, shopping, and sex? People with eating disorders still need to eat. Compulsive shoppers still need to buy things. For these, we can define abstinence as stopping the compulsive or self-destructive aspects of the behavior: Buying one watch instead of five, eating a cup of yogurt instead of a gallon of ice cream, being intimate with your partner instead of engaging in anonymous sex with others.

If your addictive behavior is of this type, you may need professional help setting boundaries, defining abstinence, and developing skills to moderate your behavior to keep it from becoming compulsive.

If you're considering the benefits of abstinence, think about this: The more years you engaged in addictive behavior and the more serious the compulsion, the more likely abstinence — rather than moderation — will help you reach your goals.

If you're thinking about moderation, here are some points to ponder:

- Programs aimed at controlled use or moderation usually recommend an initial period of abstinence. Stopping completely for a period is a healthy choice, even if moderation is your long-term goal.

- Most people find it is easier to abstain from rather than control or moderate their addictive behavior because it's difficult to know where to set the limit and then stick to it. Even people with the most committed intentions often find their behavior inches back to the point where it causes problems again.

- Instead of applying your efforts to control and moderate the addictive behavior, you can focus that energy on dealing with other aspects of your recovery.

Why you might prefer abstinence as a goal:

- It's a safe choice.

- It's simple — no counting, no precise decisions, and it's good for all situations.

- Any level of using may aggravate existing medical conditions.

- Even moderated use of a substance may worsen psychological or psychiatric problems.

- Some medications become hazardous or are rendered ineffective when combined with alcohol or other drugs.

- There may be strong social (family, friends, employer) and legal (courts) demands to abstain.

- You believe it will be easier to abstain because of your long or severe history of use, or because of background risk factors (family history, seriousness of related problems such as depression, violence, etc.).

A significant period of abstinence may:

- Enable you to find out what abstaining is like and how you feel without mood-altering substances or behaviors.

- Help you understand how you became dependent on substances or behaviors.

- Help you break other old habits.

- Allow you to experience significant life changes and build confidence.

- Please others such as your spouse, partner, children, employer, parents, and friends.

If you're considering moderation because you've tried to abstain but it didn't work, it doesn't mean you won't maintain your abstinence now. Previous attempts and lapses or relapses aren't failures. They can provide you with valuable insight if you let them.

You might be ready to abstain right now, or you may want more time to decide. Don't make that decision until you're ready. Abstinence is not a commitment to be perfect. Many people do lapse or relapse in their efforts to abstain; however, some people never do — and that may be you. Committing to abstinence means that you are committing to change. It requires patience, persistence, and practice. Breaking a commitment to abstinence is not the same as giving up on it.

You may find abstinence easy. If you have reached a point in your life in which you have had enough of the problems and disappointments from your addictive behavior, abstinence may be easier than you think. For most, however, it's more difficult than that.

Please note: If you have been drinking or abusing drugs heavily for some time and are planning to stop, consult your doctor first. It may be dangerous, even life threatening to stop "cold turkey" after a long period of continual heavy use.

You may want to do an assessment of your alcohol use. The Drinker's Checkup — **www.drinkerscheckup.com** — is a free, confidential, professionally developed and tested self-assessment. It considers many risk factors and provides measures of risk, tolerance, dependence, and consequences on several scales.

Wherever you are on this decision, you're always welcome at SMART meetings and on SROL.

Stages of Change

It's difficult to change long-standing behaviors, even when new ones are better for you. Changing addictive behavior is especially difficult because of its compulsive nature.

James Prochaska and Carlo DiClemente developed the Stages of Change model in the 1970s. They found that people who stopped smoking usually tried to stop several times before they permanently changed their behavior.

This model isn't a linear journey. Many people go in and out of different stages until they finally exit; even then, there's always the risk of relapse.

As you read each stage description below, think about which one you're in today and remember that tomorrow you may be in a different stage. For example, if you're in the preparation stage today because you're sure you want to change your behavior, tomorrow you may be in the contemplation stage because you had doubts about changing.

It's helpful if you know where you are in your recovery. Identifying the stage you're in can provide clarity in this otherwise uncharted journey into the future.

- **Precontemplation** — People at this stage usually are not intending to take action in the near future and may not be aware their behavior is problematic. Precontemplators may show up in therapy or mutual-help groups under duress — pressure from spouses, employers, parents, or courts. They resist change and usually place responsibility for their problems on external factors such as genetics, family, society, the legal system, etc. They don't feel they can do much about the situation and really don't want to.

- **Contemplation** — People start weighing the benefits and costs of change and may experience the mixed feelings — ambivalence — that people normally feel about change. Many find that writing down the benefits and costs of change help them decide (page 22).

- **Preparation** — At this stage, a person has decided their life needs to change and are open to seriously considering options. They gather information, evaluate alternatives, and take small steps toward changing their behavior. They start looking toward the future and less at the past.

- **Action** — Here's where a person takes the plunge. Action can take many forms, from the controlled environment of inpatient treatment, to working with a professional counselor, to attending mutual-help groups, to working on their own — or some combination of these. Here's where people try new ways to handle old situations, uncomfortable emotions, urges, and other challenges. This stage requires the greatest commitment of time and energy, but also is where new changes start to be visible to others. People in this stage usually need supportive relationships. They start substituting some new, healthier activities for old ones. Some people experience

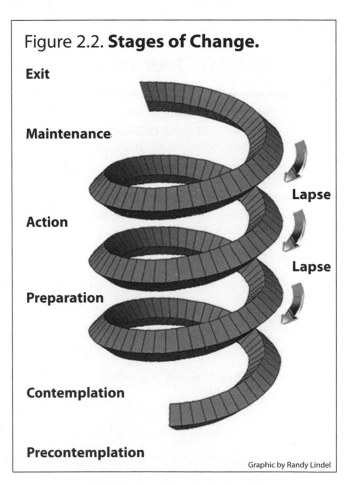

Figure 2.2. **Stages of Change.**

Exit

Maintenance

Action

Preparation

Contemplation

Precontemplation

Lapse

Lapse

Graphic by Randy Lindel

anxiety at this stage, but learn to accept a certain amount of discomfort in return for achieving their long-term goals.

- **Maintenance** — People continue building confidence as they progress on the new direction of their lives. But challenges remain; unexpected temptations may require new thinking or approaches. People usually keep seeking support from those they trust and keep doing healthy activities to cope with stress.

- **Exit** — After a long period of maintenance, most people adopt a new lifestyle consistent with their "new normal" behavior. Old, harmful behaviors no longer have a place in their lives. They express confidence and self-control, and live healthier, happier lives.

Lapse or relapse — While not a stage or necessary part of change, they are common and may occur at any stage. They are never an excuse to continue addictive behavior. If a lapse or relapse occurs, it doesn't mean a person has to restart their journey. They can identify which strategies helped them and which ones didn't, and use that knowledge to move forward with their recovery.

If you lapse or relapse, don't let it lead to crushing self-reproach and guilt. It's better to accept the temporary setback as a normal part of change and growth rather than to call your recovery a failure and give up. Handled well, a lapse or relapse can be brief and provide another opportunity for self-empowerment.

After all, when we learned to ride a bike, we fell many times before we knew how to control the bicycle.

EXERCISE: Journaling

Keeping a journal of your recovery may help you during every stage of change, in each part of the 4-Point Program® and beyond. It's a record of your progress, accomplishments, setbacks, stages, etc., and a private place to document your experiences and emotions as they happen. There are no rules to journaling.

Some people like to write in journals with favorite pens, some keep them on their computers, some use spiral notebooks, some don't like lined paper. Some people write every day as a discipline, some only write when they need to work through an issue. You can draw pictures and doodle. You may want to keep your journals forever, or eventually throw them away. It's completely up to you.

A journal of your recovery can serve many purposes. It reminds you what stage of recovery you're in, what you've been through, what accomplishments you've made, and what changes you still want to make. You can:

- Keep daily notes about what you're thinking, how you're feeling, and what you're doing.

- Break down overwhelming complex problems into smaller parts.

- Plan activities and set short-term goals.

- Identify what's helping you recover and what's not helping.

- Chart your progress along your recovery journey.

A word about privacy: Your journal is your space. You may choose to share it or to keep it private. If you're afraid to keep a journal because you think someone will read it, make it clear that your journal is off limits. You may feel more comfortable keeping it with you at all times, or finding a secure hiding place for it. Reading someone else's journal — unless you think they are in eminent danger of hurting themselves or someone else and their journal might provide information — is never OK.

Summary

Behaviors, even good ones, become addictive in nature when they become our priority, throwing our lives — and our thinking — out of balance. Addictive behavior can cost dearly in terms of relationships, careers, freedom, and independence.

Recovery is a journey in which you learn to substitute short-term gratification and irrational thinking with rational perspectives and a focus on your long-term goals. Keeping a journal can be very helpful. It's your place to record your achievements, setbacks, thoughts, and emotions.

You may be ready to commit to a life of abstinence and balance, or you may be questioning whether or not you have a problem with substance or behavior abuse. Whatever stage you're in, we welcome you to SMART.

While SMART is an abstinence-based recovery program, you may not be sure yet if abstinence is your goal. You're welcome to participate in SMART while you determine what's best for you.

Chapter 3: **Point 1– Building and Maintaining Motivation**

Why are you reading this Handbook?

Something caused you to pick up this book and at least entertain the idea of changing your life. Are you riding an emotional wave from some crisis in your life? What happens when the crisis subsides and life returns to "normal?" Will you still want to change your life?

It's easy to make a list of annual New Year's resolutions and worthy goals — lose weight, save money, become a better parent, stop this or start that. Think of the last time you made such a list. How long did it take before your life found its way back to where it was before?

So, how do we stay motivated to make the change we sincerely want? One of the biggest challenges most people face in recovery is maintaining their motivation. "Wishing" is not a reliable strategy. Some of us talk about the changes we want to make as if just talking about them will get us there.

Motivation is key to your recovery; it's what drives you to meet your goals. Without it, you're not likely to change very much. You may not realize it but you're already motivated to change. It took motivation to buy this book or to attend your first meeting, even if someone forced you. You could have said no, but you didn't. This section will help you build on those first seeds of motivation and help you stay motivated during the change process.

You may have heard that SMART is a self-empowerment program. It may sound a bit like pop psychology. It isn't. This concept is important as you prepare for the work ahead. You have power over the choices you make, how you behave, and the goals you set for your future.

TOOL: Hierarchy of Values

We all have values that motivate us, whether we've identified them or not. Chances are that you haven't recently thought about your values. The Hierarchy of Values (HOV) will help reintroduce what is most important to you.

Start by writing down as many of your values as you can think of. There are no right or wrong answers as these are very personal. When you have written as many as you can, group them into main categories, ultimately narrowing your list to five. In Figure 3.1, list them in order of importance.

Figure 3.1. **My Hierarchy of Values worksheet.**

What I value most
1.
2.
3.
4.
5.

Your list may look something like this:

What I value most
1. My relationship with my partner
2. My children
3. My physical health
4. My financial well-being
5. Personal integrity

Look over your list again. Do you notice anything missing? It's rare that a person lists their addictive behavior as a value even though it's likely the most important priority in their life. An addictive behavior can become the most important priority in your life, without you even realizing it.

Now, think about how your addictive behavior impacts each of your values. Every time you engage in your addictive behavior, you choose it over your values. You gamble with what you treasure and hold dear; you compromise your value system. A successful recovery requires sobriety to be a valued priority in your life.

When people do this exercise, they often come away with an "ah ha" moment. At one SMART meeting, a woman who was new to recovery did this exercise with the help of the facilitator. When he asked her why alcohol wasn't on her list, she burst into tears. She hasn't had a drink since!

You may now have a clearer picture of how your addictive behavior affects what you value most. These next two exercises will help you look deeper into what you want for yourself and help you identify specific and important goals you want to achieve to bring more meaning to your life.

EXERCISE: The Three Questions

Your goal is to stop using or acting out. Your desire to change is your motivation to stop your addictive behavior. It is sometimes hard to see a difference between what you *are* doing and what you could do differently to achieve your goals. This exercise can help you bring these two perspectives into focus so you can identify the discrepancy between them.

Ask yourself these questions:

1. What do I want for my future?

2. What am I currently doing to achieve that?

3. How do I feel about what I'm currently doing?

An example of answers to these questions:

1. What do I want for my future? *To be a good partner, parent, employee.*

2. What am I currently doing to achieve that? *Nothing, because I'm drunk and stoned all the time.*

3. How do I feel about what I'm currently doing? *Guilty, ashamed, depressed, frustrated, stressed, trapped.*

Now, answer the next two questions:

4. What could I do differently to achieve the future I want?

5. How would changing what I do or getting what I want make me feel?

Once you see the discrepancy between your feelings about what you're currently doing (2) and your feelings about changing your behavior (5), you can use that difference as further motivation to stop using. As you start to feel better about being abstinent, you feel more empowered to achieve your goal in #1: Be a good partner, parent, and employee.

Figure 3.2. **My Three Questions worksheet.**

1. What do I want for my future?
2. What am I doing now?
3. How do I feel about what I'm doing now?
What could I do differently to help me get what I want?
How would changing what I do or getting what I want make me feel?

TOOL: Change-Plan worksheet

Now that you identified what you want for your future and what you need to do to get there, you need a plan. In the Change-Plan worksheet, identify steps you can take toward your goal (envisioned future) and consider people who can help you get there. Create strategies to help you progress and identify signs that show you're making progress. If a strategy doesn't work, don't give up; use it as an opportunity to try something different.

You also may use this tool as a problem-solving worksheet because it can help you break large problems into smaller steps to focus your efforts so that you don't get overwhelmed.

Figure 3.3. **Change-Plan worksheet** (example).

Changes I want to make:		
Abstain within a week.		I want to eat better.
I want to be abstinent long-term.		I want to sleep better.
I want to avoid bars.		
How important is it to me to make these changes? (1-10 scale)		10
How confident am I that I can make these changes? (1-10 scale)		6
The most important reasons I want to make these changes are:		
My health is failing.		
I want my kids back.		
I want to keep my job.		
I want to have a good relationship with my ex-spouse.		
The steps I plan to take in changing are:		
Review SMART materials		
Phone my friend or go for a walk when urges get unbearable		
Buy some healthy food and try to make meals		
Fill in my time with relaxing activities		

How other people can help me:	
Person	**Kind of help**
Friend	Call me when I'm not feeling well.
Mom	Share her recipes for healthy meals.
Doctor	Monitor my overall health.

I will know my plan is working when:	
I stay sober.	I make it to work on time.
I can sleep.	I stay away from bars.
I'm eating better.	I see my doctor regularly.

Some things that could interfere with my plan are:	
Seeing a drinking friend and being pressured to go for drinks.	Isolating myself; staying inside and not exercising or eating properly.
Having a drink.	Not going to SMART meetings.

My Change-Plan worksheet   Date _____

Changes I want to make:	
How important is it to me to make these changes? (1-10 scale)	
How confident am I that I can make these changes? (1-10 scale)	
The most important reasons I want to make these changes are:	
The steps I plan to take in changing are:	

How other people can help me:

Person	Kind of help

I will know my plan is working when:

Some things that could interfere with my plan are:

TOOL: Cost-Benefit Analysis

So far, you've identified your core values and what you want your future to look like. You also have created a plan to get there. Remember, though, your addictive behavior will be waiting in the wings for the slightest opportunity to hijack your plans and motivation.

Have you ever asked yourself what you get out of your addictive behavior? You must be getting something — it's hard to imagine you'd do it if you didn't get something out of it, even if the behavior causes you or others harm.

Do you drink because it helps you cope with the stress of being a parent or the challenges of your job? Do you find anonymous sex partners to make you feel more attractive and wanted? Do you harm yourself because it calms you?

Completing a Cost-Benefit Analysis or CBA will help you answer these questions. At some point in our lives, we told ourselves — either consciously or unconsciously — that the benefits of our behavior outweighed the costs. But have you ever looked at your behavior under a microscope and really examined *all* the benefits and *all* the costs?

People who want to stop an addictive behavior have two types of thinking about their behavior, but never at the same time: Short-term thinking and long-term thinking.

Short-term thinking: Using makes you feel immediately better. Long-term thinking: You want to stop the behavior to lead a healthier life. Because short- and long-term thinking don't happen simultaneously, the CBA (Figure 3.4) brings them to one place to help you identify and compare the far-reaching consequences of your behavior with its "right now" benefits. The CBA also will help you compare long- and short-term benefits of abstinence.

To start, consider the costs and benefits of your addictive behavior.

Figure 3.4. **Cost-Benefit Analysis** (example).

Using or Doing	
Label each item short-term (ST) or long-term (LT)	
Benefits (rewards and advantages)	**Costs** (risks and disadvantages)
Relieve negativity (ST)	Hangovers (ST)
Relieve stress (ST)	Damages health (LT)
Feel more confident (ST)	Damages relationships (LT)
Socializing is easier (ST)	Divorce (LT)
Relieve physical pain (ST)	Get arrested (LT)
Makes me feel "normal" (ST)	Financial troubles (LT)
To reach a state of oblivion (ST)	Lose home (LT)
Helps me have fun (ST)	Lose family (kids, parents, siblings) (LT)

NOT Using or Doing	
Label each item short-term (ST) or long-term (LT)	
Benefits (rewards and advantages)	**Costs** (risks and disadvantages)
Improves health and hygiene (LT)	Get bored (ST)
Improves relationships (LT)	Can't relieve stress (ST)
Improves work and job safety (LT)	Have to manage pain other ways (ST, LT)
Stay out of jail/prison (LT)	Have to cope with problems (ST, LT)
Finances improve (LT)	
Won't lose home (LT)	
Won't lose my kids (LT)	
Regain self-respect, improve mental health (LT)	

The costs and benefits of using

Using the Figure 3.4 example, start by looking at what's pleasurable about your addictive behavior. Be as specific as possible. For example, instead of writing, "My addictive behavior helps me cope," write how it helps you cope. "My behavior makes me brave enough to say what I'm really feeling," or "Acting out helps me forget my loneliness."

Benefits (advantages and rewards)

- What pleasures, benefits, or advantages does it bring to my life?

- With what feelings or moods does my addictive behavior help me cope (frustration, anger, fear, boredom, depression, anxiety, loneliness, stress, etc.)?

- How does it help me cope?

- What positive feelings, moods, or situations does my addictive behavior make even better?

- What things does my addictive behavior help, or at least seem to help me do better?

- Does it help me avoid reality or escape?

- Does it ease or reduce physical or emotional pain?

- Does my addictive behavior help me socialize and fit in?

- Do I need my addictive behavior to seem more fun, charming, interesting, or more confident?

- Do I need my addictive behavior to feel normal?

Costs (risks and disadvantages)

- What is it that I dislike about using?

- How is it harming me?

- What will my life be like if I continue to use?

- How much time have I lost to my addictive behavior?

- How many people do I lie to in order to hide my addictive behavior?

- How do I feel after the effects my addictive behavior wear off?

- How is using affecting my health?

- Does using affect my energy, stamina, and concentration?

- How much money have I lost to my addictive behavior?

- What legal problems do I face because of my behavior?

- How does using affect my relationships?

- How does using affect my work performance?

- What effects has it had on my self-respect and self-confidence?

The costs and benefits of not using

Now, do the same exercise for your life without addictive behavior. Be honest and realistic.

Benefits

- How will stopping affect my health?

- How will stopping affect my relationships with the ones I love?

- How will stopping affect my job?

- How much money can I save?

- What will stopping do to my self-respect and self-confidence?

- Will stopping affect my ability to deal with my problems?

- What will I do with the time freed up because I'm not pursuing my addictive behavior?

- What goals have I abandoned that I could accomplish?

Costs

- What will I miss about using?

- What issues in my life will I have to find new ways to deal with when I stop using?

- What thoughts and emotions will I have to learn to accept?

- What will change about my life that I like now because I use?

My Cost-Benefit Analysis

The substance or activity to consider is: _____

Date:_____

Using or Doing	
Label each item short-term (ST) or long-term (LT)	
Benefits (rewards and advantages)	**Costs** (risks and disadvantages)
NOT Using or Doing	
Label each item short-term (ST) or long-term (LT)	
Benefits (rewards and advantages)	**Costs** (risks and disadvantages)

Short- and long-term benefits

Once you have your list of benefits and costs for each section, identify each one as either short-term benefit or long-term benefit.

Are you surprised that most of the benefits of using and costs of stopping are short-term while the costs of using and benefits of stopping are long-term? In SMART meetings, we often hear gasps from people as they realize their addictive behavior has only short-term benefits but long-term costs. This may be the first time you've taken a hard look at the price you — and those around you — have paid for your behavior.

Now that you're considering your behavior in terms of immediate and lasting benefits, the decision whether to use or stop is clearer.

Keep your CBA handy and refer to it when you have an urge. Make copies and keep them within easy reach. Make it a living document: Revise and update it whenever you need to.

The CBA is a great tool to use for any change or decision you want to make.

Summary

So far, you've done some wonderful — and difficult — planning. Congratulations. You identified your values, what you want your future to look like, what's important to you, and how your current behavior undermines your goals.

You made a plan to create your future and honor your values, and you identified your support system — the people who can help you along your journey. You also identified, possibly for the first time, the long- and short-term costs and benefits of your addictive behavior.

These are powerful insights. You may find yourself referring to these pages to help you stay motivated, especially as you move into Point 2: Coping with Urges.

Chapter 4: **Point 2 – Coping with Urges**

Now that you're committed and motivated to change your behavior, let's look at how you can deal with any urges you may have to use. Learning to cope with urges is the difference between abstaining and using. It can be difficult. The feelings can be intense, and you're used to giving into them. It takes strong mental and emotional commitment on your part to change these patterns.

Some people report having no urges after they make the choice to stop. Some report they have urges later on. Dealing with them may be mentally difficult; it may be physically and emotionally uncomfortable, but it's not impossible. You can do it.

According to Webster's Dictionary, an urge is an action "to press; to push; to drive; to impel; to force onward." It also says an urge is "to press the mind or will of; to ply with motives, arguments, persuasion, or importunity."

Urges are psychological in nature and not the physiological withdrawal symptoms you may experience when you first stop using (behavior or substance). However, resisting urges may cause physical or emotional discomfort.

The more you know about urges and understand why they happen, the better equipped you are to cope with them. Rather than an excuse to escape into your addictive behavior, you'll be able to use urges as a catalyst in your emotional growth.

You can learn to recognize urges without acting on them. The more you do that, the easier it gets. Most people who recover from addictive behavior say that, after a while, the urges go away completely as they replace the unhealthy behavior with healthy alternatives. In the first few days and weeks of your abstinence, your urges may be very strong and may grow stronger for a while.

Scratching an itch

If you've ever had a rash from poison oak, poison ivy, chicken pox, or allergies, you know how intense the itch can be. It feels like the only relief from the discomfort is to scratch — long and hard. Scratching the rash may make it feel better short-term, but the long-term consequences are slower healing, permanent scarring, and vulnerability to infection.

There are other ways to cope with the itching. At first, soothing remedies such as anti-itch cream and oatmeal baths don't seem as satisfying as using your fingernails, but they produce the long-term benefits you want: to be rash free with no lasting scars.

In that same way, you may feel like the only way to stop an urge is to use. But like the itch, there are healthier ways to cope, even though they may not seem as immediately gratifying.

Learning to cope with your urges enables you to achieve your long-term goals. There's no way around this.

Beliefs about urges

It's likely that you've been feeding your urges for so long that you don't even think about them. They feel like they're part of who you are.

You may hold beliefs about your urges that are unrealistic or untrue, and that actually make them worse. When your beliefs about urges are accurate and true, it's possible to ease them or even prevent them.

Here are some opposing beliefs about urges that may help you understand them:

- **Unrealistic**: *My urges are unbearable.*
- **Realistic**: Urges are uncomfortable, but you can bear them. If you keep telling yourself that you can't bear them, you're setting yourself up to use. Urges won't kill you or make you go crazy; they'll just make you uncomfortable.

- **Unrealistic**: *My urges only stop when I give in.*
- **Realistic**: Urges may last only seconds to minutes, but rarely much longer. Sometimes urges come in batches, several shorter ones rather than one long urge.

  - Urges always go away. Here's why: Your nervous system eventually stops noticing stimuli. If it didn't, you couldn't wear clothing because it would be too uncomfortable. If you fast, you know hunger eventually fades away. The dentist-office smell that was so strong when you walked through the door isn't even noticeable by the time you leave.

  - You can teach yourself to ride out urges. It does get easier over time.

- **Unrealistic**: *My urges make me use.*
- **Realistic**: Using is always a choice. When an urge hits, you have two choices: to use or to ride it until it subsides.

- **Unrealistic**: *Urges are a sign that my addictive behavior is getting worse.*
- **Realistic**: They're a normal part of recovery. They may be stronger at first — or maybe later in your recovery — but they weaken, and eventually disappear. You *can* have a life without urges.

- **Unrealistic**: *Giving in to an urge isn't harmful.*
- **Realistic**: Giving in to urges prolongs their presence in your life because it reinforces the behavior pattern. It will make stopping harder as the next urge will likely come more quickly and be more intense.

  - Like the rash, if you scratch it occasionally but use healthy remedies the rest of the time, the occasional scratching still increases the healing time.

  - If you occasionally give in to your urges, you simply prolong your dependence on the substance or behavior as a way out when you believe the pain is unbearable.

  - What happens when a child nags for hours for a new toy and you say no until you tire of their whining and say yes just to get them to stop? You stop the immediate whining, but you teach the child that if they whine long enough, you'll give in. In the same way, you strengthen your urges every time you make the choice to give in to them, even if it's just occasionally.

- **Unrealistic**: *I must get rid of urges.*
- **Realistic**: Your urges are normal. Addictive behaviors cause changes in your brain that make urges very powerful, so "getting rid of them" is an unrealistic expectation.

  – You can't control urges, but you can control how you respond to them.

  – It takes time and practice to replace old thoughts and behaviors with new ones. Don't expect urges to end immediately, don't expect to be perfect, and don't give up.

- **Unrealistic**: *I'm self-destructive or I wouldn't do these self-destructive things.*
- **Realistic**: Our brains are hard-wired to seek out things that provide pleasure. Substances and behaviors that light up the pleasure centers in our brains can be destructive if the desire for them turns into a need. Oh, and as human beings, we all do stupid things.

- **Unrealistic**: *I use because I like to.*
- **Realistic**: While that was probably true in the beginning, it's probably more complicated than that now.

  – While using continues to light the pleasure centers in your brain, your rational brain can't ignore that the short term "pleasures" are incompatible with your long-term goals. With more exploration, you will probably find that you have fallen into the "addictive behavior trap," in which you ignore the benefits of stopping because you may be preoccupied with how difficult it will be.

  – SMART's tools and strategies give you an edge in dealing with your urges. The tools and strategies — along with your motivation — can make it possible for you to successfully cope with urges.

EXERCISE: Identifying your triggers

What is a trigger?

Triggers are the things that lead to cravings (*I want to*), which can lead to urges (*I need to*). They may be your emotions; something you've done, are doing, or want to do; a time of day, week, or year; something you touch, hear, see, smell, or taste; or anything else that leads to urges. Each of us has our own triggers.

They are not excuses to use and they are not unpredictable.

Addictive behavior teaches your brain to associate some things with the pleasure or relief you feel when indulging in the addictive behavior. Even when you stop, your brain will be reminded about the addictive behavior when you encounter your triggers, or allow yourself to conjure up triggers.

Your brain can unlearn this thinking reaction (*I want to*) to a trigger. These reactions may last a while but will eventually decrease to be the briefest (milliseconds) of unhelpful thoughts. As humans, brief, ridiculous, and unhelpful thoughts come into our heads all the time about things we quickly dismiss for what they are — silly thoughts and no more. The more serious urges (*I need to*) usually subside in a few days, weeks, or months.

To identify your triggers, think about the substances or behaviors that stimulate your senses: Sight, smell, hearing, taste, and touch (Figure 4.1). Make a list. You may not be aware of how many there are. How many can you identify? Be honest and list them all, even if they seem insignificant.

Figure 4.1. **Identifying triggers** (example).

Addictive behavior	Trigger examples
Heroin	Seeing needles and drug paraphernalia
Sex	Provocative ads, perfume, certain hairstyles
Cocaine	Any white powder, tin foil
Food	Grocery shopping, potlucks, certain aromas
Alcohol	Ads, sound of a can opening, certain times of day
Gambling	Lottery ads, seeing scratch games in store, football pools
Marijuana	Certain music, skate parks, seeing rolling papers in store
Smoking	Meals, smell of cigarette smoke, stress, coffee or alcohol

Identifying my triggers

Addictive behavior	Trigger examples

Trigger risk

Once you identify your triggers (and you may identify more as you continue your recovery), keep track of how likely the triggers are to spark an urge. The highest-risk triggers are those that most often spark an urge for you.

Rate each trigger from 1-10 (10 is the riskiest or most likely to trigger an urge). This will help focus your efforts so you can work on the hardest triggers first.

Figure 4.2. **Trigger risks.**

Trigger	Rate risk on 1-10 scale
Unpleasant emotions: Anger, frustration, grief, etc. Others:	
Pleasant emotions: Joy, peace, anticipation, etc. Others:	
Unpleasant physical sensations: Pain, cold, heat, etc. Others:	
Stress: Peer pressure, work issues, general fear, financial concerns, etc. Others:	
Conflict with others: Spouse, co-worker, boss, children, parents, etc. Others:	
Physical place or time: Restaurant, park, with friends, car, work, summer, evening, etc. Others:	
Other:	
Other:	

Now that you rated the risk of each trigger in Figure 4.2, apply the triggers to your addictive behavior. For each addictive behavior, list every situation you can think of that triggers your urge to use. Start with the riskiest (10) to the least risky (1). Follow this example:

Figure 4.3. **Trigger worksheet** (example).

My addictive behavior: Cocaine	
Trigger:	**Risk: 1-10**
Fighting with my spouse	10
Hanging out with Robert	10
Driving by the corner where I used to buy	8
Dancing at a nightclub	3
Holidays	10

My trigger worksheets

My addictive behavior:	
Trigger:	**Risk: 1-10**

My addictive behavior:	
Trigger:	**Risk: 1-10**

Urges

Identifying your triggers is an important part of your recovery. Awareness gives you the power to understand and deal with urges; however, even with awareness and planning, you will experience urges. It's a normal and natural part of recovery.

An awareness and understanding of urges is crucial to recovery. You identified what triggers them, but do you know how long they last? How intense they are? How frequent? Most people with addictive behaviors don't realize that urges usually last only seconds to minutes and then pass.

One way to understand your urges is by recording them in an urge log.

EXERCISE: Urge log

An urge log (Figure 4.4) is a table in which you record specific information about your urges. After a few entries, you may notice patterns and similarities about your urges. The log then becomes a road map that will help you anticipate situations and emotions that may trigger

Figure 4.4. **My urge log.**

Date	Time	Rate 1-10	Length of urge	What triggered my urge?	Where/who was I with?	How I coped and my feelings about coping	Alternative activities, substitute behaviors
8/29	1:15	8	1 minute	Having lunch in winebar	Lisa and Stephanie	Told them; I forgot about it pretty fast	Avoid having lunch there

urges. You also may notice certain thought patterns associated with your urges, which are helpful in self-management and problem solving (Point 3).

You may find that you can create an urge log in your journal, if you're keeping one. If you're not, use Figure 4.4 (there's another blank one in Appendix B). Keep it with you so you can immediately log each urge before you forget it. At first, you may need to write in it many times a day.

When you identify urges triggered by certain times, places, or situations that you encounter regularly, you can plan ways to avoid those triggers or, distract yourself from the urge until it passes.

See Figure 4.4 for an example of the log.

Distracting yourself

Although it may be difficult at first — especially during intense urges — distracting yourself is one of the best ways to get through an urge. When you're actively doing something, you're thinking about that and not the urge.

The more you refuse to give in to urges, the less frequently they occur, and the more quickly they pass. They also will become less intense.

See Figure 4.5 for examples of activities you can use to distract yourself from an urge.

Figure 4.5. **Identifying distractions.**

Category	Activities
Chores	Clean, cook, wash dishes, iron, garden, laundry
Exercise	Walk, run, swim, yoga, Pilates, ski, weights, inline skate
Games	Computer, board, cards, chess, puzzles, darts
Arts	Draw, paint, write, photography, sculpture
Crafts	Knit, embroidery, leather work, scrapbook, wood work
Martial arts	Aikido, judo, karate, tai chi, tae kwon do, jujitsu
Outdoor activities	Bird watch, walk, hike, bike
Performing arts, music	Sing, play, practice music, mime, dance
Personal growth	Read, attend a meeting, career development
Read, listen	Fiction, nonfiction, music performance
Social activities	Invite a friend out, attend a MeetUp, group or club
Spectator	Go to a movie, live theater, watch TV, old movies
Team sports	Table tennis, hockey, soccer, softball, kickball
Academics	Art, history, language, math, science, humanities
Trades and crafts	Paint, build, work on car, tinker in your garage
Vent feelings	Talk, journal, draw, cry, throw eggs at the ground
Volunteer	Soup kitchen, hospice, church, SMART

Take a moment to identify distractions that would be helpful to you.

My distractions	

Consider using the Weekly Planner (Figure 4.6) to document your interests and activities. Plan activities for times you know you may get urges. Check your urge log or trigger worksheets for times when urges tend to strike.

STRATEGY: Coping with urges

On the following pages is a list of basic and advanced strategies adapted from Dr. Tom Horvath's book *Sex, Drugs, Gambling & Chocolate: A Workbook for Overcoming Addictions*. You can practice and refine these so that they work best for you. The first 14 are the easiest to learn and do. The advanced strategies require deeper self-knowledge and more practice. It's important to discover which ones work for you and then practice them frequently. After a while, you won't need to practice them because they'll become part of your life; you won't even have to think about them.

Basic strategies

1. **Avoid** — Stay away from the triggers that lead to urges. Avoid situations, sensations, or stimulations that may bring on an urge. The earlier in your recovery that you identify high-risk cues that trigger urges, the earlier you can start avoiding them or escape when unexpectedly faced with them (strategy 2).

2. **Escape** — Get away from the urge-provoking situation. If you find yourself there, leave immediately.

3. **Distract yourself** — Concentrate on something other than your urge. Distract yourself with activities you enjoy, especially if the urge is intense. Simple activities, such as counting objects or saying the alphabet backward, can fill up your attention so that you have nothing for the urge. Focusing on your Hierarchy of Values is a positive form of distraction.

4. **Develop coping statements** — Instead of thinking, "I deserve a drink because I have to deal with X problem," tell yourself, "Even though it sucks that I have to deal with X problem, drinking isn't going to help me."

5. **Review your CBA** — It may not turn off the discomfort, but it may help you maintain your motivation to resist your urge. It may help to review it regularly, even when you're not having an urge.

Figure 4.6. **Weekly planner.**

Time	Monday	Tuesday	Wednesday	Thursday	Friday	Saturday	Sunday
Morning							
Midday							
Evening							

6. **Rate your urge** — Write in your urge log. Put it in perspective and look for exaggeration. On a scale from one to 10, rate its intensity. Are you exaggerating? Compare the discomfort of resisting the urge to other uncomfortable things, such as being boiled alive or having your fingernails pulled out.

7. **Recall moments of clarity** — Think of a moment when you realized using was a problem for you, or a moment when you knew that changing your addictive behavior was, without question, the right thing for you to do.

8. **Recall negative consequences** — When you feel an urge, you may think only of the benefits of using. To create a more accurate picture, carry the thought through to include the negative consequences that follow. For example, if you've given up smoking and a cigarette urge arises, you may fantasize about how good it feels to inhale the smoke. Carrying that thought through means you also remember how badly you cough when you walk up a flight of stairs.

9. **Picture your future** — Visualize yourself in the near future feeling good about resisting the urge. For example, paint a mental picture of getting up early Saturday morning without a hangover.

10. **Use the past** — Recall successfully resisting urges in the past. Remind yourself that the urge will pass and how you have routinely resisted them.

11. **Ride the wave** — Observe the urge and visualize that you are surfing a wave that grows, crests, weakens, and disappears.

12. **Call on role models and coaches** — Talk to others who have mastered coping with their urges to learn from their experiences. SMART meetings and the SROL message board and chat room are filled with people farther along in their recovery who are willing to encourage and support you.

13. **Reach out for social support** — Talk with a nonjudgmental and supportive person. It's helpful to have a list of people you may call when you're feeling the discomfort of an urge. Let them know how they can help you because they may not intuitively know.

14. **Accept the urge** — Recognize that it is uncomfortable and hold it at a distance. Experience it as you would any passing thought. Observe it as an outside object. See it but don't evaluate it. Acknowledge it as something that used to be a problem, then return your attention to whatever you were doing. Don't turn the urge into a bigger issue by pretending it doesn't exist.

Advanced strategies

1. **Move beyond avoidance** — When you're in the early stages of recovery, it's wise to stay away from places that trigger urges whenever possible. Avoidance, however, is not a realistic long-term strategy. Eventually, you'll be in a situation in which someone will offer you a drink, drugs, etc. You need to have the confidence to resist such offers.

   It may help to bring along a trusted companion for support and guidance.

   • Put yourself in a situation that may trigger an urge, such as a restaurant that serves alcohol.

   • Use whatever basic strategies (1-14) have helped you resist urges.

- Practice refusing offers of your addictive behavior so that you can handle peer pressure. Visualize:

  – Someone trying to persuade you to use, or making fun of you if you refuse.

  – Yourself confidently refusing.

  – Someone who stirs strong emotions in you and is intent on getting to you to use.

  – Keeping your focus and managing your responses.

2. **Bring out your urges** — After you develop some mastery of coping with urges, you may want to confront them on your terms rather than wait for them to happen. It may help you gain confidence in your ability to cope with them. To bring out urges:

   - Visualize a past situation in which you had a strong urge.

   - Allow yourself to feel the urge and visualize giving in to it. Let it pass.

   - Now, visualize the same situation again, only don't give in to the urge this time.

   - Do this for as many situations as you need to.

   - Using the same technique, rehearse a situation that may happen in the future.

3. **Role-play / rehearsal** — SMART meetings are safe places to role-play. Other people act the parts of the people you anticipate will challenge you in high-risk situations. The meeting facilitator can help set up a role-play.

   Here's a sample:

   - Show your role-play partner how you think a difficult person will behave.

   - Your partner plays the difficult person while you play yourself in the situation.

   - Once you finish the scenario, swap roles, and do it again.

   - The people watching the role-play can then show you how they might handle the same situation differently by playing your part.

   Consider role-playing challenges associated with events like holiday parties, weddings, and other special events.

4. **Refuse to use in social situations** — There will always be occasions to use or act out. How do you deal with them? Here are some ways:

   - Talk with a fellow recovering or recovered person about an upcoming event that you think may trigger an urge; a party, for example. Update them afterward.

   - Bring it up in a SMART meeting.

   - Rehearse or role-play the event with a SMART group and by yourself. Role-play or visualize the whole event. Prepare answers to the questions people will ask. Visualize getting a soft drink. Do it in your mind until it becomes natural.

   - If the host is a friend, tell them before the event that you aren't drinking. Enlist them as an ally.

   - Take a more experienced nondrinker or a friend with you who knows your situation.

- Eat something before the event, especially if you don't know when, or if, you'll be able to eat again.

- Arrive late; leave early. Prepare and use an escape plan. If necessary, prepare reasons for leaving early.

- Upon arrival, immediately get something nonalcoholic. You can then socialize with a glass in your hand not feel like you're standing out. This forestalls the "Can I get you something?" awkwardness.

- Remember, your drinking or not drinking is less important to others than you think. It's unlikely anyone is watching you or focusing on you for long.

If someone insists that you use:

- Make eye contact. It shows you're serious.

- Speak in a firm, unhesitating voice.

- Don't feel guilty. You have the right not to use.

- After you say no, change the subject. You only have to say no once.

STRATEGY: Defeat urges with DEADS

You can knock down urges DEADS! This is an easy way to remember strategies when faced with an urge. Urges can muddy your cognitive abilities, making it hard to think clearly. DEADS can help you think clearly about how to deal with the urge, no matter how intense.

- **D = Deny / Delay (Don't give in to the urge)** — Remind yourself, repeatedly if necessary, this urge will pass. Refuse to give into it — no matter what!

- **E = Escape the trigger** — If you know what is causing the urge, leave immediately.

- **A = Avoid the trigger** — You can keep track of when you get urges using the urge log (Figure 4.4). Urges can occur routinely as part of your daily pattern. If you know you will be in a situation that triggers an urge, plan to avoid the situation. The earlier in your recovery that you identify high-risk stimuli that trigger urges, the earlier you can avoid those situations or escape when unexpectedly faced with them.

- **A = Attack the urge** — Dispute irrational beliefs (DIBs, page 46) and obsessive thoughts, or do an ABC (page 39). Practice relaxation or meditation (page 67).

- **A = Accept the urge** — Tell yourself the urge will pass soon and that if you don't give in to it, the next urge will be less intense, and they will become less frequent. You may want to sit quietly by yourself to surf the urge: feel it build then fade while you acknowledge your thoughts and feelings about the urge, the present, and your future. Remember, don't turn the urge into a bigger issue by pretending it doesn't exist.

- **D = Distract yourself with an activity** — Do something: go for a walk, read a book, or watch TV. If you're putting your mind on something else, then it can't focus on the urge. Simple activities, such as counting objects or saying the alphabet backward also can fill up your attention. Do something, even if you don't want to (clean the fridge, walk the dog). Motivation may follow the action.

- **S = Substitute for addictive thinking** — Send in healthy substitute thoughts to squeeze out the urge:

  - Replace an irrational belief (*This urge will kill me*) with a rational one (*This urge is bad but it won't kill me and it will pass*).

  - Substitute feeling down and alone by going to the gym or stopping by the SROL chat room.

Figure 4.7. **DEADS worksheet.**

Identify your strategies for successfully coping with urges.

D = Deny / Delay (Don't give in to the urge)

- How long do urges last if you don't give in? How bad do they get before fading? What can you quickly do that will help you deny them?

  _____

  _____

  _____

E = Escape

- What triggers can you get away from? What can you do to escape a trigger's influence?

  _____

  _____

  _____

A = Avoid, accept or attack

- What can you do to avoid urges?

- What techniques or strategies have helped you "to be" with the urge until it passes without giving in? How do they make you feel and think that is different from how you think and feel when you're not having an urge?

- What tools or words can you use to attack the urge?

  _____

  _____

  _____

D = Distract yourself with an activity

- What activities have you considered, written down, or done to take your mind off the urge and to fill the time that you used to spend on your addictive activity?

  _____

  _____

  _____

S = Substitute for addictive thinking

- What thoughts can/have you developed to dispute the illogical thinking that comes with urges?

- What healthy activities can you do to replace down thinking and feeling?

  _____

  _____

  _____

Thinking Strategies

TOOL: Destructive Images and Self-talk Awareness and Refusal Method (DISARM)

In the same way that your addictive behavior is only a behavior and not "you," an urge is merely a feeling or an impulse you experience, not the essence of you.

Some people find it helps to cope with their urges if they give them a name, as if the urges were another being or something outside themselves.

Give your urge and its voice a name that describes what it feels like when the urge comes on. SMART participants have used names like, "The Inner Brat," "The Lobbyist," "The Whiner," and simply, "The Enemy."

Naming your urge may help you recognize it sooner. When you hear the first whispers of its voice, address it by name, and firmly refuse it. Tell it to get lost or that it's no longer welcome; laugh at it. Then visualize it getting smaller and weaker, and disappearing.

Personifying your urge helps in two ways: It serves as a reminder that you are not your behavior; it defines something that, until now, may have felt amorphous and shadowy. It puts you in a power position over the urge and your addictive behavior.

Dealing with discomfort

Discomfort of any type, emotional or physical, can go hand-in-glove with urges. As we explained in chapter 1, it's our beliefs about an event and our resulting discomfort that can influence our addictive behaviors.

Your beliefs can be a major source of discomfort. At some level, you may believe that you can't survive discomfort or shouldn't have to tolerate it. Thinking about it in this way may actually cause it to intensify.

Abstinence will be difficult if you refuse to accept mild or temporary discomfort as a normal part of life. If you've spent years escaping from discomfort through your addictive behavior, you've built up powerful habitual responses to it. Now you have the opportunity to accept and deal with discomfort in healthy ways. Remember, before your addictive behavior began, you dealt with discomfort without the behavior. You can learn how to do this again.

Some situations are not what you want them to be. Discomfort can be a useful feeling that tells us something is not right and motivates us to change the situation, or our thinking about it. Discomfort is not always "bad"; it is sometimes just part of the human condition.

What is discomfort?

Distress and discomfort manifest themselves in the body in different ways:

- **Physical pain** — It's not just the pain but our demand that such pain must not exist that leads to additional discomfort.

- **Withdrawal and rebound** — When you stop an addictive behavior, you may experience withdrawal or rebound. For example, if your addictive behavior gave you relief, you may experience despair or depression. The discomfort may feel intense for the first few weeks; however, be confident that it will eventually decrease.

- **Anxiety** — Sometimes people experience anxiety after withdrawal and rebound. This type of discomfort may be what propelled you into your addictive behavior in the first place. Evolution tells us that we may have inherited some anxiety or uneasiness from our ancestors. It kept them vigilant against the dangers of a wilder and more uncertain world. Anxiety is stronger in some people than in others, but it's natural in all of us. We add to our anxiety and discomfort by believing that the world must be safe and that we must control everything.

- **Depression** — Biology and heredity can be a major contributor to clinical depression that requires medical treatment; however, much sadness and situational depression is a result of the demands we place on ourselves, on others, and on the world. If you believe that you must be loved or must be successful to be happy, you will likely find yourself unhappy much of the time. Others may believe that they don't deserve happiness because they are unworthy of it. You don't have to get the things you demand to be happy. Your sense of worth is too complex to be judged by others.

- **Frustration and anger** — If you see yourself as doing things badly, doing things that aren't in your best interest, or see others as treating you unfairly, you're probably going to feel some discomfort. The pursuit of self-confidence may leave you feeling uncomfortable because you may believe you must perform well all the time. Dictating the way others should act can inevitably lead to frustration when they choose not to act the way you want. You will feel all shades of frustration, anger, or even rage when these demands are not met or you think they won't be.

TOOL: The ABCs for coping with urges

Dr. Albert Ellis addressed the above distress-producing beliefs in his book *A Guide To Rational Living*. He suggested that people feel the way they think. He used the ABCs of REBT (Figure 4.8). By learning this technique, you can develop a life skill that will help you think and feel better, and more consistently with what you desire for yourself long-term.

An ABC will help you identify and work through your thoughts and feelings about a specific issue or event that causes you discomfort. Doing an ABC takes effort and can be difficult at first. You may want to do your first one in a SMART meeting to get the hang of it.

Figure 4.8. **ABCs of Rational Emotive Behavior Therapy.**

- **A – Activating event:** The starting point of your discomfort, for example, your boss yelled at you. The result is you feel an unhealthy emotion — "unhealthy" in that it triggers you to behave in a self-defeating way. A cues B.

- **B – Beliefs about the event:** You hold irrational demands and demonstrate low-frustration tolerance — *I can't stand it*-itis — about feeling this discomfort:

  - *I must (get drunk, get high, overeat, gamble, act out) to cope with how mad I am at my boss.*

  - *If I don't, I won't be able to stand these feelings.*

- **C – Consequences of your beliefs:** Because of your beliefs about the event, you feel even more emotional discomfort. This builds on the urge to engage in addictive behaviors to feel better. These emotions and behaviors are the consequences of B (*I'll show her. I'll leave early to get drunk.*).

  - **NOTE:** You may find it easier to begin the ABC by identifying the unhealthy consequences first (*I lapsed and started drinking*), then identify the activating event (A) and the irrational beliefs (B) you held about A that got you to C.

  - The B-C connection. What has more influence over how you feel and want to act now, the activating event or your irrational beliefs about the event? If you chose B, you're right! This is the essence of REBT. You may not be able to change A, but you can control your beliefs about it. If you change how you think about A, you'll change how you feel about it and how you react.

- **D – Dispute your beliefs:** Identify your irrational demand and low-frustration tolerance beliefs in B and dispute them by asking if they're true: *Even though it's uncomfortable feeling like this, do I have evidence that I must get drunk to cope?*

- **E – Effective new belief:** You can replace irrational beliefs with rational thoughts. Identify what you want that you have turned into a rigid demand does not make sense. Also identify that not getting what you want will not kill you so it's not unbearable:

  - *I really want to use when I feel like this but I don't have to and I don't need to feel better.*

  - *It's unpleasant and uncomfortable to feel like this until the discomfort and urge pass, but it won't kill me. I can stand it and it isn't unbearable.*

When you understand that these new and effective beliefs are true, your discomfort subsides or decreases, reducing the urge's intensity.

Figure 4.9. **ABC for coping with urges** (example).

Activating event	**B**elief about the event — irrational	**C**onsequence of irrational belief	**D**ispute the irrational belief	**E**ffective thinking change
The event that created the urge.	What I believe about **A**. Find the irrational demand — the MUST.	How I feel and how I behave as a result of **B**.	A more helpful belief about **A** that replaces the irrational belief.	How I feel and act as a result of **D** — my new rational belief about **A**.
My boss yelled at me today in front of my co-workers.	*He shouldn't yell at me! He has no right to embarrass me in front of my peers! It's not fair!*	*I'm really mad and I want to stop at the bar for a drink on my way home!*	*Who says my boss shouldn't yell at me? He yells at my co-workers a lot. Who says life is always fair?*	*While I don't like to be yelled at and feel upset, this guy yells at everyone. He's not worth giving up my sobriety!*

In chapter 5 we'll learn more about ABCs.

My ABC for coping with urges

Activating event	**B**elief about event — irrational	**C**onsequence of my irrational belief	**D**ispute my irrational belief	**E**ffective change in my thinking
The event that created the urge.	What I believe about **A**. Find the irrational demand — the MUST.	How I feel and how I behave as a result of **B**.	A more helpful belief about **A** that replaces the irrational belief.	How I feel and act as a result of **D** — my new rational belief about **A**.

Summary

We pointed out a few ideas in this chapter. First, urges will be part of recovery for most people. In the past, you may not have thought that acting on an urge was a choice. Now, you've learned that urges are opportunities to make choices — engage in an unhealthy behavior to make the discomfort of the urge go away, or choose to deal with the urge in ways that will help you achieve your long-term goals.

We dispelled some common myths around urges that may have locked you into bad choices because you didn't have any better information. Now you do. We also explored some tools that can help you deal with urges when they arise and even build up your resistance by exposing yourself to controlled urges — much like a vaccine builds your ability to fight disease.

If you practice and rehearse the strategies that work for you — at home and at meetings — you will likely succeed at not giving into urges. Try them all and use the ones that work best for you.

Making the choice to not use when you have an urge is an important step in learning how to manage your thoughts, feelings, and behaviors.

Chapter 5: **Point 3 – Managing Thoughts, Feelings, and Behaviors**

In chapter 1 we introduced you to this basic concept of REBT: Many of our behaviors are influenced by the way we see the world. Like our addictive behaviors, our thinking also can become automatic. These habitual thoughts can lead to feeling emotional discomfort, so we turn to our addictive behavior to feel better.

Managing thoughts

In this chapter, we'll guide you through techniques that can help you change your automatic thinking patterns. As you begin to think about the world differently, your emotions and behaviors also will change.

The philosophy of unconditional acceptance

Adopting unconditional acceptance can be a key to overcoming emotional problems associated with addictive behaviors. This also can be a life skill that will help you long after your addictive behavior is behind you.

Unconditional acceptance is something we already know, but for it to become a personal philosophy, you may have to learn to recognize your unhelpful beliefs you automatically hold when unpleasant or unexpected things happen in your life. Once you spot these in your thinking, you can then remind yourself of more helpful ways to think.

This starts with reminding yourself that you are human. As such, you know that you aren't perfect and that you'll make mistakes, do some things badly, and do some bad things. This is all a normal part of being human; making mistakes and failing is how we learn.

As human beings, it's normal to exaggerate events that involve us.

When you find yourself automatically thinking negative thoughts, or exaggerating and judging how bad you are, remind yourself of your humanity and of those traits that we all share. By identifying unhelpful thoughts and replacing them with more accurate and helpful thoughts of acceptance, you'll feel better and want to act in healthier ways. After practicing this for a while, more accurate thinking will become automatic for you. Like most things, though, it takes practice.

Downing beliefs

We commonly hold on to downing beliefs in which we put ourselves, others, and our lives down. By doing so, we may end up feeling guilty, ashamed, depressed (*I messed up again — I am a total failure*), or angry (*He treated me badly — he's a total jerk*). These inaccurate and exaggerated downing beliefs can lead to the powerfully distressing feelings that can trap you in a cycle of addictive behavior.

You can choose to replace downing beliefs with these acceptance principles:

I accept myself because I'm alive and have the capacity to enjoy my existence. I am not my behavior. I can evaluate my behavior, but it is impossible to accurately and honestly evaluate the complexity of my "self."

I strive for achievement only to enhance the enjoyment of my existence, not to prove my worth.

Failing at a task doesn't make me a failure. I can choose to accept myself even if I am unwilling or unable to change my character defects, because there is no law of the universe that says I can't.

My self-approval cannot come from pandering to an external source or bowing to any external authority. My self-acceptance can only come from within me, and I am free to choose it at any time.

— *Nick Rajacic, MSW, SMART Facilitator*

Unconditional self-acceptance (USA)

Unconditional self-acceptance is the idea that you have worth, just as you are. This explains what separates "you" — your character, traits, personality, strengths, and weaknesses — from your behaviors. This is why SMART doesn't use labels. You may have addictive behaviors but you are *not* an addict. While this might seem like a game of words, it's important to recognize how powerful words and labels are.

The same labels that you may carry internally — "failure," "disappointment," or "loser" — led to your unhealthy behaviors. Attaching new labels won't help.

If you can't accept yourself, can you really expect others to? Even if they do, would you believe them?

Accepting yourself may be difficult. You may have caused others and yourself extreme harm and pain. You may have ruined the lives of others, plunged your family into debt, brought diseases into trusting relationships, or squandered your life savings. Who can forgive that? Not everyone can, but you can forgive yourself and accept that you are a worthwhile person in spite of your past behaviors.

Be patient with and kind to yourself. Be honest about what you've done. Accept that you can't change the past, but you can create your future.

You may be tempted to compare yourself to others or hold yourself up to some arbitrary standard. There is no standard or universal measure of your value. You stand alone in your self-worth.

Comparing yourself to others is as meaningless as judging one color against another: Is red good or bad? Is blue more valuable than green?

Unconditional other-acceptance (UOA)

You may judge other people inaccurately and in an exaggerated way, just as you judge yourself. Once you accept that other people are capable of making mistakes, then you can accept that they may fail at things, too. Judging another as totally bad — no matter how badly they treat you — is as exaggerated and as damaging as making the same judgment about yourself.

Unconditional life-acceptance (ULA)

You can judge life in the same way, as being completely unfair or totally terrible. When you find yourself thinking, "Life sucks! It couldn't be more awful!" Remind yourself of the good things that have happened in your life.

If you can accept that there are many things you can't control, it may help you to better accept what life throws at you, even if you don't like it.

Rational and irrational beliefs

Beliefs people have about themselves and about the world come in two categories:

1. **Rational** – They're true, make sense, or are helpful.
2. **Irrational** – These are untrue, don't make sense, or are harmful.

The list below is some of the common types of irrational beliefs associated with negative feelings that fuel addictive behaviors. Do you recognize any?

Demands: Must, have to, and should beliefs are absolutes that put unrealistic demands on you, others, and life. Have you ever said, "I have to succeed at this," "They should not have done that to me," or "My life must be better than this"? All of these rigid demands will lead to emotional distress when they're not met or we believe they won't be.

Over-generalizations: Only, always, and never beliefs also are absolutes — all or nothing — with no room for options. Do you ever say, "You always screw up," "My addictive behavior is the only way I can cope," or "Things never go the way I want them to"? Believing absolutes eliminates any room for variation, and life is filled with gray areas and unknowns, even if you'd rather it wasn't.

Frustration intolerance: I can't stand, I can't handle, and I can't deal with beliefs are generally false. Have you ever said, "I cannot stand this aggravation," "I cannot handle the pressure of my new job," or "I cannot deal with your nagging"? The truth is, you *do* stand, handle, and deal with, although not always in healthy ways.

Awfulizations: Worst thing ever, horrible, awful, and adjectives ending in -est (meanest, laziest, cruelest, nastiest, etc.) beliefs exaggerate how bad things are. For example: "This is the worst thing that's ever happened to me," "She's the cruelest boss on earth," or "That driver is absolutely horrible." Is what happened to you really the worst that's ever happened? How many times have you applied that very belief to unpleasant situations in your life? Awfulizing may have been one of your excuses to use.

Irrational and unrealistic beliefs tend to come easy to us. Take time to examine what you're thinking, and ask yourself, "Is this belief really true? What is the evidence that supports it? What is a more balanced belief for me to hold about this situation?"

EXERCISE: Disputing Irrational Beliefs (DIBs)

You can use this tool to examine any belief that may be harmful if you act on it.

An irrational belief (IB) is:

- **Not true** — It's unrealistic and there is no evidence to support it, or it

- **Doesn't make sense** — It's not logical, or it's

- **Harmful** — It won't help you get what you want for yourself in the long run if you act on it.

A rational belief (RB) is:

- **True** – It's realistic and there is evidence to support it, or it

- **Makes sense** – It's logical, or it's

- **Helpful** – It helps you get what you want in the long run if you act on it.

Disputing irrational beliefs

You can dispute an IB by turning it into a question and then answering it. Your answer will probably be a RB.

Example IB: I will just have one drink and then quit.

- **Question the IB**: Will I just have one?

- **Answer**: I may, but probably not. I never just have one. I'll just get drunk again, get in a fight, get arrested, and my wife will likely leave me (RB).

Example IB: This urge is unbearable and I can't stand it!

- **Question**: Is this urge unbearable?

- **Answer**: No. It's really unpleasant but it won't kill me. I can stand it, therefore, it's not unbearable (RB).

Using the table in Figure 5.1, identify some of your IBs that lead to emotional distress and wanting to use or act out.

Figure 5.1. **Disputing Irrational Beliefs** (example).

Irrational belief	Question IB	Rational belief
I always fail.	Do I always fail?	I have done some useful things in the past so I don't and won't always fail.
I'm totally worthless.	Have I never done anything worthwhile?	I have done some worthless and useless things BUT because I have had success at things, I cannot judge myself as a totally worthless person.
My partner treats me unfairly. He is a bad person.	Does my partner treat me unfairly? Is he a bad person?	He has done unfair things BUT he also has done many things to help me so I can't judge him as a totally bad person. No one is perfect.
Nothing good ever happens to me and never will.	Does nothing good ever happen to me?	The love and support of my family and friends are all good things that continue to happen to me.
I must always do whatever it takes to be comfortable.	Is it realistic to expect to always feel comfortable?	Comfort ebbs and flows. It may be better to stay uncomfortable temporarily if it will help me achieve my long-term goals.
When I mess something up, it proves what I have always thought: I am a complete failure.	Am I a complete failure?	I don't judge others as harshly as I judge myself. Everyone makes mistakes. I can make mistakes and learn from them; it makes me human, not a failure.
I have to be better and do better than the people around me or I am nothing.	Am I really nothing?	I don't need to prove I'm better than others to be OK. I can be happy just as I am, and deserve to accept myself.
Because my addictive behavior has proven that I'm a loser, I should never trust myself and my instincts, and will always need the advice of others.	Do I need others' advice?	I've made mistakes and will continue to make them. BUT I can trust my thoughts and feelings, and I don't need to rely on others' opinions to validate my self-worth.
Others are responsible for my unhappiness. I hate them, I want to punish them, or I complain bitterly when they disappoint me.	Are other people in charge of my happiness?	*I'm* responsible for my happiness. Holding others responsible is unrealistic, unfair to them, and doesn't lead to my long-term happiness.
I must find the one person or belief that will make my life stable.	Is there one person or belief that will make me happy?	Life is an ongoing process of learning many things and relating to many people. It's a journey on which I will change and grow.
I'm bored, and that makes me uncomfortable. The only thing I can do is engage in my addictive behavior.	Is using the only option I have?	I can do other things to relieve the boredom. If I do one, I will be less bored and it will get my mind off my addictive behavior.

What are some of your beliefs that commonly come up when feeling distressed or when you have an urge to use? Write them down then turn them into questions. Then answer the questions to develop more helpful beliefs.

Disputing my irrational beliefs

My irrational belief	Question my IB	My rational belief
I can't cope with stress without using.	Can I cope without using?	It may be hard, but it won't kill me and it will get easier.

STRATEGY: Change your vocabulary, change your feelings

Because your feelings are influenced by your thoughts, you can change your feelings and behaviors by changing your thoughts. And you can change your thoughts by changing the words you use in your thinking. The difference that changing just one word makes might surprise you. The more you do this, the more natural it becomes. Figures 5.2 – 5.4 show some examples and include space to write your own.

Figure 5.2. **Word exchange.**

Instead of saying or thinking:	Say or think:
Must	Really want / prefer / choose to
Should	Really want / prefer / choose to
Have to	Want to
Can't	Choose not to
Ought to	Really want / prefer / choose to
Awful	Not great / undesirable
Unbearable	Unpleasant
Can't stand	Don't like
Always	Often
All	A lot

Figure 5.3. **Statement exchange.**

Instead of saying or thinking:	Say or think:
I must be perfect	I really want to do well
You should not do that	I prefer you not do that
You ought to help	I would appreciate your help
I can't stand this feeling	I don't like feeling this way
You are a bad person	I don't like your behavior
This urge is awful	This urge is unpleasant
This situation is unbearable	This is not the best way
Everything is terrible	Things are not the way I want them to be
This happens every time	This frequently happens
I need your love	I want your love
I'm a bad person	I behaved badly
I am a failure	I made a mistake / I failed at

Figure 5.4. **Emotion vocabulary exchange.**

Instead of saying or thinking:	Say or think:
I am terribly anxious	I feel concerned
I am so depressed	I feel sad
I am really angry	I feel annoyed
I am guilty	I feel remorse / I feel regret
I am so ashamed	I feel disappointment
I'm really hurt	I feel sorry
I'm jealous	I feel concern for my relationship
I'm envious	I feel unhappy

Managing feelings

Strong emotions are an inevitable part of the human condition. You can learn to reduce unhealthy negative emotions (unhealthy because these make us want to behave in self-defeating ways) and even change them to healthy negative emotions (healthy because they can help us get what we want for ourselves in the long run).

Let's use anger as an example. Some low-level annoyance or aggravation — healthy anger — can lead to positive and assertive action: standing up for yourself or others in the face of injustice. Rage — unhealthy anger — can be dangerous and destructive, leading to negative and aggressive behavior. While annoyance is balanced by logic, extreme anger — as with any intense emotion — reduces your logical brain's ability to control your behavior. You may start thinking that extreme anger and aggression are justified, and end up getting into serious trouble.

Learning to reduce or change excessive emotions will make it easier to change how you act.

TOOL: The ABC for emotional upsets

The ABC helps reduce or change an unhealthy emotion about an event by changing your beliefs about the event (Figure 5.5).

As you may remember from chapter 4, doing an ABC takes effort but when successful, you'll be better able to deal with problems, and you'll have another life skill that will be with you long after you have put your addictive behavior behind you.

Working through an ABC

Start with your most distressing emotion about an event or the one associated with an urge. It's important to deal with just one emotion and one emotional goal at a time.

1. **Find the C and A**

   - Initially, you'll find the emotional and behavioral consequences at C.

     – How do you feel or how were you feeling?

     – What did you want to do or what did you do?

   - Emotions do not just happen on their own. There is always a situation that accompanies an emotional problem. We call this the "activating event." It can be a situation, person, place, thing, or thought.

   - Within the activating event, there is usually one thing that is the most distressing about the event. Often this is a negative and inaccurate evaluation of what we find to be the event's most distressing aspect.

   - To find the activating event (the A), ask yourself:

     – What happened to make me feel this way?

     – What was the single most distressing thing about it?

2. **Identify the emotional goal at E**

   - What is the healthy emotion I will work toward?

     – Annoyance instead of rage; acceptance instead of "should"; concern instead of jealousy, etc.

3. **Find the irrational belief at B**

   - The A and C can get you to your belief B if you ask:

     – *What am I telling myself about the A that makes me feel and want to act this way?*

     – *What demand am I making of myself, others, or life? If this demand is not met, is it truly awful, or am I putting myself, others, or life down?*

4. Dispute your irrational belief and find helpful belief at D

- Dispute your IB using DIBs (page 46): Turn your IB into a question. Your answer will be your new rational belief:

    - *It's his fault I feel this way! Are my feelings his responsibility?*

    - *I just know she's cheating on me! Do I have evidence that she is?*

- If you find an irrational demand at B, show yourself that the demand is unrealistic:

    - *I accept I may not* (rational belief) **instead of** *I must succeed* (irrational demand).

    - *I know I can't control her behavior* (rational belief) **instead of** *she must be nicer to me* (irrational demand).

- You also can add any anti-awfulizing, frustration tolerance, and acceptance beliefs if you find any attached to the demand. For example:

    - **Anti-awfulizing** — *Good things do happen to me* (rational belief) **instead of** *nothing good ever happens to me* (irrational belief).

    - **Frustration tolerance** — *I don't like those dogs in my flower garden so I'll talk to their owners about it* (rational belief) **instead of** *if those dogs don't stay out of my flowers, I will kill them* (irrational belief).

    - **Acceptance** — *He can be very loving so judging him as totally bad is unfair* (rational belief) **instead of** *he is a complete jerk because he gets mad at the littlest things* (irrational belief).

5. Adopt new beliefs – E – to feel the healthy emotion

This will take practice and you may have to work at it a lot until you feel the beliefs to be true. Once you complete the ABC, run through it in your mind many times to consciously feel differently about the event.

Figure 5.5. **ABC for dealing with emotional upset** (example).

Activating event	**B**elief about the event — irrational	**C**onsequence of irrational belief	**D**ispute the irrational belief	**E**ffective thinking change
The event that created the emotional upset.	What I believe about **A**. Find the irrational demand — the MUST.	How I feel and how I behave as a result of **B**.	A more helpful belief about **A** that replaces the irrational belief.	How I feel and act as a result of **D** — my new rational belief about **A**.
I'm bored and have absolutely nothing to do tonight.	*I HAVE to relieve this anxiety right now or I'll explode. Using will help me feel better, and I deserve to indulge myself.*	*I'm really anxious because I know I can't cope without using when I'm bored.*	*Will I really explode? No. Using won't help me achieve my long-term goals nor will it help me learn how to deal with this emotion.*	*My long-term goal is so important that I will not use. I'll meditate or take a walk to replace anxiety with healthier, less intense feelings.*

My ABC for dealing with emotional upset worksheet

Activating event	**B**elief about event — irrational	**C**onsequence of my irrational belief	**D**ispute my irrational belief	**E**ffective change in my thinking
What happened?	What am I telling myself about the event? Example: Demand, awfulizing, downing, frustration intolerance, etc.	How does my irrational belief make me feel? Example: Rage, depression, anxiety, shame, avoidance, aggression, etc.	Turn **B** into a question (DIBs). Example: *Am I really a...?; Do I have proof of ...?*; etc.	Rational thoughts, moderate emotions. Example: Annoyance, disappointment, assertiveness, sadness, etc.

Figure 5.6. **Replacing excessive emotions.**

Excessive emotion (at C)	Healthy emotion (at E)
Anxiety	Concern
Depression	Sadness
Rage	Annoyance
Shame	Regret
Guilt	Disappointment
Hurt	Disappointment
Jealousy	Concern, disappointment

STRATEGY: Coping statements during a crisis

When you're in a crisis, an ABC probably won't be very helpful because it takes time and rational thought. Simple and easy coping statements will help you get through a crisis. They are simply statements you say to yourself to get through the moment until you have time to do an ABC. Work through an ABC when you're emotionally detached, not in the heat of the moment.

It's most helpful if you develop and rehearse several coping statements so that they're ready when you need them. For example, "This is frustrating, but I can live through it," "I'm hurting, but using will make me feel worse."

Make your coping statements realistic without putting demands on yourself or others. You can use a copy of the worksheet provided for the Disputing Irrational Beliefs exercise (page 47) to come up with and keep a list of your own rational coping statements handy.

Below are some of examples of coping statements.

To improve frustration tolerance:

- *I'm frustrated. I don't like this, but it won't kill me. I can handle what I don't like without shooting off my mouth and saying something I'll regret.*

- *This is upsetting, but I can stand what I don't like.*

To calm an angry rage:

- *I'm really annoyed. It's OK to feel this way and I don't have to act on my feelings.*

- *I don't have to lose it when someone acts badly toward me. It's OK to feel annoyed.*

To curb anxiety and depression linked to self-judgment:

- *I can't change what happened so I'm not going to let it get to me.*

- *I made a mistake. I'm human. I forgive myself so I can move on.*

You can find more coping statements in Bill Borcherdt's book, *Think Straight, Feel Great!: 21 Guides to Emotional Self-Control*. There also is a list of coping statements on SMART's website.

Each time you replace irrational harmful thinking with rational helpful thinking, you feel better and want to act in ways that reflect your feelings.

Solving life's problems

When you take an addictive behavior out of your life, you will still have your share of difficulties, but without the extra problems and complications the addictive behavior adds. One life skill we can all use is problem solving — breaking down paralyzing problems into smaller, manageable steps.

Managing problems becomes easier once you accept that:

- There will be people who will never accept that you have changed.

- There are and always will be some situations that are beyond your control.

You may have acted out because problems overwhelmed you and you saw no solution except escape through your addictive behavior. A big part of managing thoughts, feelings, and behaviors is finding a way through life's problems rather than around them. Having a more positive outlook and accepting things for what they are can save you a lot of trouble and worry. By stubbornly refusing to let your emotions take over, problem solving gets easier.

Remember the three Ps: **Practice, Patience, Persistence**.

EXERCISE: Five steps of problem solving

Consider using this model for solving problems:

1. **Define the problem.** You can't solve a problem that you haven't defined. It's a common human trait to assume we know what the problem is, then jump to conclusions and solutions.

   - Some problems are so large they can't be solved until you break them down. You can't solve world hunger, but you can feed a homeless family.

   - Defining a problem involves two steps:

        a. Understanding its specific nature, and

        b. Identifying workable solutions.

     – If your problem is finding a new place to live because you've been evicted, the solution is straightforward. If your problem is a teenage daughter who keeps running away, it may take time to define the root problem, and even longer to solve it.

2. **Brainstorm.** Come up with as many solutions to the problem as you can. You can do this alone, with a friend or therapist, or in a SMART meeting.

   - The secret is to let ideas flow without judging or discussing them. Be wild; push the envelope. Be open to all ideas.

   - Do this until you run out of ideas. The main rule is don't analyze or judge the ideas. Don't let anyone say, "That won't work," or, "I tried that once and ...." during brainstorming. Ideas, even bizarre ones, may stimulate your thinking, and lead you to ideas that can work. Let them build on each other. You'll assess them in the next step.

3. **Evaluate:** Use a scale from zero to 10 to rate each idea:

    - How realistic is it?

    - How likely is it to work?

    - Does the solution have rewards?

    - What are the consequences?

    - Can I afford it?

    - If an idea scores zero, throw it out, but be careful not to judge too quickly. An idea that seems unworkable or too "out there" at first may look more reasonable the longer you think about it. If you have assumptions about any of the ideas, you may need to gather more information before you rate it to determine if your assumptions are true or false.

4. **Select:** You've evaluated and rated your ideas. Now select one and try it. What's most important is that you have thought through your choices, something you may not have a lot of experience doing.

5. **Create a written plan**: You'll most likely get better results if you write down your plan instead of just carrying it around in your head.

    - Write down the solution you choose, and how you will implement it. Write the start date and location, and everything you'll need to make the solution successful. You can use the Change-Plan worksheet (page 18) for this.

    - Put your plan into action!

Record your results every day if appropriate. Is your plan working? Did you modify it? Compare your results with your expectations. It's likely that your results are different from what you wanted or expected. Can you adjust your plan? Should you try a different solution?

Ask others for their ideas, or discuss it at a SMART meeting. Getting quick feedback on your plan will help you stay focused on solving your original problem.

Like most things in recovery, this takes practice. Like all skill building, it helps to find people who will give you honest feedback while supporting you. You'll make mistakes; you'll get discouraged. Don't give up, and don't label yourself a failure. With time and effort, healthy problem solving will become second nature to you.

STRATEGY: Relapse prevention

You'll recall from chapter 2 that a lapse is a short slip into old behaviors. Relapse is a prolonged return to your old way of life. A drunken night versus a months-long return to using alcohol, for example.

If you consider yourself recovered, watch out for complacency. Remember where you have been and what you have achieved — forever. You will need to think carefully and honestly about how vulnerable you may still be, and be appropriately vigilant.

A period of abstinence also may lead you to think you have "regained control" and can now re-engage in moderate use. Beware of this thinking; it's an excuse to use. Doing an ABC on

"I've regained control" thinking may help you maintain your motivation and prevent lapses or relapses.

Body systems have memory, so even if you're abstinent for a long time then lapse or relapse, you may engage in your addictive behavior with more intensity. This is called the abstinence violation effect.

SMART considers lapses and relapses as temporary setbacks in recovery. If you have a lapse or relapse, you can learn from it. Use it to develop more strategies to avoid another one.

Danger situations

A lapse or relapse can happen without having an urge. There are six danger situations that may set you up for this. Recognize them so you can be prepared.

You may prepare for them by going over your core values, goals, and developing a plan for these situations.

The danger situations are:

1. **Association** — Exposure to something that was a trigger in the past or being in situations in which you used in the past.

2. **Boredom** — The discomfort of boredom may bring up old thinking patterns.

3. **Emotions** — Strong emotions may catapult you into old coping methods.

4. **Fantasy** — Romanticizing the fun parts of your addictive behaviors.

5. **Frustration** — Like other strong emotions, frustration may hurl you backward to old ways of coping.

6. **Opportunity** — A time when there is seemingly no down side to acting out, and no one will know but you. Opportunity is a powerful enticement.

Remember, the best way to handle a lapse or relapse is to prevent it; active intervention measures can be successful. If the thought that you want to engage in the old behavior hits you but is not an overwhelming urge, you can simply ask yourself if acting on your thought is a good long-term choice. Any of the techniques mentioned in Point 2: Coping with Urges, will help you think about such cravings more realistically. Just use the techniques that have worked for you before. Although lapses and relapses are common, they don't have to be common for you.

Here are some other tips to help you avoid falling back into unhealthy behaviors:

1. **Get medical and psychological help** for emotional or mental illness, and take medications as prescribed.

2. **Live with awareness** of the PIG (page 6) and of consequences for lapses and relapses. Carry, review, and update your CBA or a list of reasons for sticking to your change plan.

3. **Stimulus control.** Avoid, escape, or change the activating events, cues, or triggers for using that you can avoid, escape, or change.

4. **ABCs.** Continue to work on changing irrational beliefs that may bring on a relapse.

5. **Reward yourself** for continued abstinence and compliance with treatment.

6. **Substitute activities** for your old behaviors. Develop a balanced life with occasional healthy indulgences that can substitute for the unhealthy behaviors. Discover and create other interests (next chapter).

7. **Distractions.** Relaxation, meditation, exercise, art, reading, talking with people who support you, etc.

8. **Irrelevant decisions.** Be mindful of seemingly irrelevant decisions you may make that put you in high-risk situations. Recovery requires living with greater awareness.

9. **Abstinence violation effect.** Don't use a lapse as an excuse to relapse.

10. **Lapses and relapses can be opportunities for growth.** They don't prove you're a failure or that you're locked into your destructive behaviors forever. Regard them as a normal but undesirable possibility. Take it seriously, figure out why it happened, and find new strategies to avoid repeating the error.

Summary

By learning to manage your thoughts, you feel better. When you feel better, you behave in ways that reflect your feelings. Developing more rational thinking through practice and use of the tools and strategies in this chapter will help you temper or change the strong emotions that, in the past, led you to act out. In the past, thinking irrationally, experiencing excessive emotions, and acting in ways that reflected those feelings were automatic, so thinking, feeling, and behaving in new, more rational ways can become automatic, too.

Chapter 6: **Point 4 – Living a Balanced Life**

Regaining your health and creating a lifestyle that brings you long- and short-term satisfaction is an important part of recovery. Avoiding lapses and relapses, and achieving long-term behavior change is supported by living a balanced life. Balance comes from finding and pursuing interests that you find absorbing, and achieving your short- and long-term goals.

A meaningful life is one that is in balance; you now have the time and desire to pursue the activities that express the values you identified in the Hierarchy of Values. Many people do not live their lives in balance, nor in a manner that consistently sustains their values.

It's important to note that achieving a balanced lifestyle is just like the other points in our 4-Point Program — it takes work. You can use many of the SMART tools in your quest to achieve and live a balanced life. The tools aren't just recovery tools; they are tools for life.

There are two main actions that lead to a balanced life:

1. Understand and respect each of the areas of your life.

2. Change your perspective in the areas in which you are stuck.

EXERCISE: **Creating balance**

Eating right, getting enough sleep, relaxing, and meditating will help you restore balance to your life. Let's look at the other areas of your life.

In this exercise to create balance in your life, you'll:

1. **Take an inventory.** When completing the Lifestyle Balance Pie in Figure 6.1, you'll determine and evaluate the areas to focus your time and energy on.

2. **Be honest.** This exercise will show you the areas in your life that may need more or less of your attention. When you're done filling out the pie, be honest with yourself about your reaction to the picture it shows. What are your thoughts and feelings? Are there areas in which you want to spend more time? Are fears or discomforts keeping you from doing something? How would you start filling out the neglected areas? When would you begin?

3. **Go with your gut.** When looking at your pie, you may find several areas that you feel could use more attention, and you probably don't have time to work on all of them at once. Which one is waving its hand wildly and saying, "Me first! Pick me!" Follow your instinct. It's easier — and more fun — to work on the area you're drawn to first.

4. **Plan and prepare.** To pay more attention to the neglected areas, you'll need to make time for them, otherwise they won't get done. Focusing on these less-tended areas will take some getting used to. Create a plan that you can stick to.

5. **Get support.** Making changes isn't easy. Rather than struggling and risking failure, get all the outside help and support you can. You might ask loved ones, friends, colleagues, or seek professional help.

6. **Balance.** Your pie may show that you spend a lot of your time in one area at the expense of others. How much time do you spend on the things that are going well for you? Again, be honest. Is it that specific area that you spend the most time on? All of the areas in your life should be done with moderation and balance in mind. Otherwise, your life becomes unbalanced and one-sided.

7. **Have fun.** If the work you put into balancing your life starts to feel burdensome, back off a bit. You are doing this work to become healthy and whole, not to add more chores to your life. Seek out the fun in all your efforts; have a good time with the new experiences while exploring the other areas of your life. When your life becomes more balanced and well-rounded, the healthier and happier you'll be.

Lifestyle Balance Pie

Use the Lifestyle Balance Pie in Figure 6.1 to represent the different areas in your life.

1. Label each slice with an area of your life that is important to you. For example, family, friends, spirituality, romance, health, work, recreation, personal growth, money, physical surroundings, etc. Refer to your HOV on page 14 for insight.

2. Think of the pie's outer edge as being completely satisfied (10) and the center as being very dissatisfied (0).

3. Rate your level of satisfaction in each of the areas you've listed by placing a dot on the middle line of each pie slice to indicate the level of satisfaction you have in that area.

4. After you rate each slice, connect the dots to create the outside perimeter of your pie. What does it look like? Is it round and full or does it look like some areas are not as filled out as others?

5. Now ask yourself:

   – Are my true values and priorities reflected here?

   – Based on what I see, am I living a balanced life?

   – Am I involved in too many activities? Is there too much on my plate?

   – How much of my time is spent caring for others? For myself?

   – What area(s) needs more attention? What needs less attention?

   – Is there a dream or desire that I'd like to focus on?

   – What changes do I want to make? What can I do to "round out" my life?

To move yourself toward a more balanced life, allow yourself more time for the areas that show gaps — those places where pieces of your pie are missing (because they are). When doing so, be sure to focus on the whole picture of your life, not just specific areas.

Figure 6.1. **Lifestyle Balance Pie** (example).
This exercise and graphic is based on the work of Julia Cameron's
The Artist's Way, and is used by permission
from Penguin Publishers.

Lowest scores	
Life category	**Score**
1. Leisure fun	2
2. Health	2.5
3. Finances	4.9
4. Volunteering	5
Highest scores	
4. Children	6
3. Marriage	7.5
2. Career	9
1. Education	10
Plan	
My "Leisure Fun" and "Health" slices got the lowest scores. To increase both, I will join a walking club on MeetUp, which will help me kill two birds with one stone: Have fun and improve my health through exercise. When I'm confident that I'm committed to these goals and see improvement in both areas, I'll focus on "Finances," my next lowest score.	

While the goal is never to neglect any area, his top four scores probably don't require the focused attention his bottom scores do.

Idea: Because "Health" covers such a wide variety of topics, he could do a Lifestyle Balance Pie just on that life category — exercise, nutrition, sleep, blood pressure, cholesterol, doctor's appointments, etc.

My Lifestyle Balance Pie

Date _____

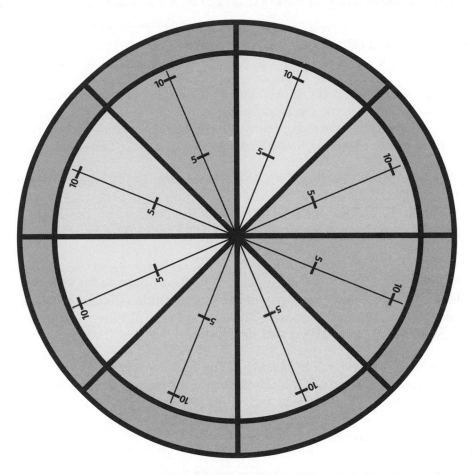

Lowest scores	
Life category	**Score**
1.	
2.	
3.	
4.	
Highest scores	
4.	
3.	
2.	
1.	
Plan	

TOOL: Vital absorbing creative interest (VACI)

Before your life was overtaken by addictive behavior, there were probably hobbies and activities you enjoyed and others you wanted to try. Now you can bring them back into your life, and explore the new ones. Hobbies and interests help balance your life.

A vital absorbing creative interest can help bring the simple pleasure of living back into your life. When we get overly involved in any one activity, be it helpful or not so helpful, we cut a lot out of our lives that we used to enjoy. Finding a balance can restore the fun and enjoyment that life has to offer. So, how can we get back to those simple pleasures of life?

First, look at the benefits list on your CBA. What were some of the benefits you were getting from your addictive behavior before the costs became too high? Did you enjoy the buzz? Did you like being able to just check out for a bit? Was it the taste or the social aspect? Believe it or not, each of these benefits is a key to finding a VACI.

If you enjoyed the buzz, then look at things you could do to get a real buzz out of life. The reward will be greater and you will remember it in the morning and for years to come. Maybe you decide to ride a roller coaster you have never ridden before. Maybe it's taking up running or race walking. Perhaps you have always wanted to sky dive or ride a motorcycle. Figure out what would give you a buzz and take it on.

If using or acting out allowed you to "check out" for a bit, maybe looking at some ways of being away from the world for a while might give you the chance to restore your energy. Take a walk by yourself. Go to the ocean and watch the waves. Go on a day trip and be alone with yourself in your car. A bike ride is a great way to be alone with nature. What about gardening, crafts, and artistic endeavors?

Be careful to do your VACI in moderation so that you don't replace one addictive behavior with another.

If you leaned on alcohol or drugs to help you feel comfortable in social situations, you might challenge yourself to go to a social event and act as fun and as friendly as you were when you were using.

What did you like to do as a kid? What hobbies did you have? What dreams were never realized? Now is the time to take your life back and make some of those things happen.

Variety is the spice of life. Find many VACIs and keep looking for more. Life is full of amazing and new things to learn and do.

VACI list

Use the table in Figure 6.2 to make a list of the VACIs that interest you. Write it down then rate it, 1-10, on how much it interests you. After you try it, come back to the list and rate it again to see how closely your "before and after" ratings are.

Figure 6.2. **VACI 'before and after' list.**

VACI	Before 1 – 10	After 1 – 10	Comments/thoughts

Setting goals

So far in this chapter, we've helped you identify what parts of your life are probably in need of your attention: regaining your physical, mental, and emotional health; and rediscovering lost passions and interests, and creating new ones. You also identified, in the Lifestyle Balance Pie, the areas that are important to you and which ones might need a little more work.

Putting this all together requires planning, flexibility, creativity, and energy. But, where to start? Setting goals. Goals help you maintain your focus on achieving balance and direct your energy toward your new life and away from your old one.

Like many who suffer from addictive behaviors, goal setting may be unfamiliar to you. Now that you have freed up the time you used to spend engaging in addictive behavior, you have time to focus on your values and interests.

The goals you set will be more meaningful if you connect them to your values. You may want to review your Hierarchy of Values from Point 1. Using your values as your guide will help you set priorities and point your new life in the direction you want it to go.

EXERCISE: Values, goals, and planning

Establishing values and goals, and creating plans and strategies to achieve those goals are essential to all aspects of recovery, especially when creating a balanced life. Our values guide our lives, from the long-term goals we set to the day-to-day choices we make.

Consciously defining and living your core values are empowering because your values are the essence of who you are. Your values may include honesty, fidelity, reducing your environmental footprint, not eating meat, honoring your elders, parenting based on love instead of fear, etc. If honesty is one of your values, then one of your goals might be, "If I have a lapse, I will tell someone as quickly as I can"; or "I will be honest with my children about my past."

Planning will help you achieve your goals. While most of us probably haven't done a lot of planning (we were too focused on immediate gratification), it's a crucial skill to learn. If you're committed to telling the truth about a lapse, write down how you would do that and whom you would tell. "If I lapse, I will tell my best friend"; "If my child asks about my past drug use, I will tell them what I believe is appropriate without glorifying my behavior."

You'll hear people in SMART talk about the three Ps: patience, practice, and persistence. We could add a fourth one: planning. It's that important.

Where to start

Setting a few short-term goals is great starting place. You can set long-term goals after you set some that will benefit you now. Make sure your goals are realistic without being too hard, and don't set too many.

Based on your HOV, what are the areas of your life you want to improve? Here are some ideas to get you started:

- **Finances** — Save more money? Pay off bills? Donate to charity (maybe SMART perhaps)? This might be one of your first goals if your financial situation is what motivated you to get help.

- **Friends and family** — Improve relationships? Make new friends who are sober? Spend more time with your children? Many in recovery make this their first goal.

- **Career** — Find a new job? Improve a skill at your current job? Get some on-the-job training to advance?

- **Physical health** — Rebuild muscle tone? Walk around the block without wheezing? Go vegetarian? Get more sleep? Tending to your physical health will improve your mental health, too.

- **Fun and leisure** — Bowling? Model trains? Shark fishing? Cooking? Astronomy? On the road to recovery, boredom can be a dangerous sinkhole. Rediscovering old hobbies and interests or learning new ones can help you avoid falling into it.

- **Artistic activities** — Singing? Embroidery? Glass blowing? Sculpting? Self-expression through the arts boosts self-confidence.

- **Education** — Finish your degree? Take classes for fun? Make yourself more marketable? As you know, you can always learn new things. Taking courses at a community center, community college, or university will help keep you engaged in life and learning.

- **Volunteer** — SMART? Hospital? Child's school? Charities? Animal shelter? Election campaign? You may feel a desire to give back as part of your new life. Volunteers are in short supply everywhere. Finding an organization that is in line with your values is uplifting, rewarding, and a great place to make new friends.

- **Social activities** — Ballroom dancing? Book club? MeetUp groups? Church? Because most of your past social activities probably revolved around your old addictive behavior, learning to socialize in new ways may take determination.

Setting realistic goals

Goals should be:

- **S**pecific — "Run a marathon" vs. "Improve my cardio health"
- **M**easurable — "Go to bed at 10 p.m." vs. "Get more sleep"
- **A**greeable — "I'm invested in this goal" vs. "I *should* do this because ..."
- **R**ealistic — "Train for next year's marathon" vs. "Run marathon next month"
- **T**ime-bound — "Volunteer five hours a week" vs. "Donate to charity"

Here are three practice goals to help you see the process.

Figure 6.3. **Goal setting.**

Example goal #1.

Life category (from Lifestyle Balance Pie): Physical fitness				
Related to value (from HOV): Health				
Goal: Improve cardio endurance				
Specific	**M**easurable	**A**greeable	**R**ealistic	**T**ime-bound
		✓	✓	
Revised goal (if needed): 5k Walk for the Cure				
Specific	**M**easurable	**A**greeable	**R**ealistic	**T**ime-bound
✓	✓	✓	✓	✓
Tasks/objects to reach goal: Walk four times a week until race (12 weeks)				
Week 1: 20 mins	Week 2: 30 mins	Week 3: 30 mins	Week 4: 35 mins	Week 5: 35 mins
Week 6: 40 mins	Week 7: 45 mins	Week 8: 50 mins	Week 9: 60 mins	Week 10: 60 mins
Week 11: 60 mins	Week 12: 30 mins	End of week 12: Walk for the Cure!		

Example goal #2.

Life category (from Lifestyle Balance Pie): Physical fitness				
Related to value (from HOV): Health				
Goal: Eat better for the rest of the year				
Specific	**M**easurable	**A**greeable	**R**ealistic	**T**ime-bound
				✓
Revised goal (if needed): Lower blood cholesterol to 180 in six months				
Specific	**M**easurable	**A**greeable	**R**ealistic	**T**ime-bound
✓	✓	✓	✓	✓
Tasks/objects to reach goal: Eat red meat once a month, eat fish three times a week. Eliminate hamburger and bacon. Make tuna fish sandwiches for lunch twice a week. Make one new healthy fish recipe a week for dinner. Follow doctor's recommendations. Regular cholesterol screenings (per doctor's orders).				

Example goal #3.

Life category (from Lifestyle Balance Pie): Relationships				
Related to values (from HOV): Living authentically; my children				
Goal: Show up for all visitation sessions (and be on time) for next 3 months.				
Specific	Measurable	Agreeable	Realistic	Time-bound
✓	✓	✓	✓	✓
Revised goal (if needed): Not needed				
Tasks/objects to reach goal: Create electronic calendar with reminders of all visitation sessions, March – May.				
Leave one hour before visitation to be on time (to account for traffic, road construction, etc).				
Talk to boss Wednesday to schedule the time I need off March – May.				

Now it's your turn. There are more goal setting tables in Appendix B.

My goal setting.

Life category (from Lifestyle Balance Pie):				
Related to value (from HOV):				
Goal:				
Specific	Measurable	Agreeable	Realistic	Time-bound
Revised goal (if needed):				
Specific	Measurable	Agreeable	Realistic	Time-bound
Tasks/objects to reach goal:				

Other goal-setting tips

- Choose the categories in which you want to set goals.
- Don't set so many that you get overwhelmed.
- Write down each goal, and include what you need to do to meet each goal.
  - To stay on track, create weekly "To Do" lists with all of the tasks that you need to do each day to meet your goals.
- Review your list at the end of the week.
  - Check off the tasks you finished.
  - Move unfinished tasks to the next week's list.
  - Repeatedly unfinished tasks may indicate that you're not as invested in the goal as you thought, or the goal simply needs fine-tuning.

Living with emotions

Strong emotions are an inevitable part of the human condition. As we discussed in "Point 3: Managing Thoughts, Feelings, and Emotions," learning to level out your emotions is helpful in managing behavior and also can be part of living a balanced life.

Emotions reside on a spectrum. One end is general well-being and emotional balance. Here, logic and emotion complement each other. Think of Yin and Yang.

The opposite end of the spectrum is extreme, intense feelings: bursting happiness, debilitating depression, homicidal rage, etc. The closer you get to the extreme end, the less likely you will be thinking rationally and the harder it will be to balance any of your emotions and behaviors.

Learning to balance feelings and rational thought is important to achieving a more balanced life.

Awareness techniques

Many people recovering from addictive behaviors find themselves preoccupied with thoughts, prone to ruminating, or easily caught up with strong feelings such as cravings.

Learning to pay attention to the present moment and becoming more "mindful" can improve well-being and lifestyle balance. Mindfulness is the opposite of mindlessness. It describes a state of active, nonjudgmental attention to the present.

Originally a form of Buddhist meditation, there has been a lot of research into mindfulness techniques. They are shown to reduce depression, obsessive thinking, stress, anger, and even post-traumatic stress. Emerging evidence suggests it helps people in overcoming addictive disorders.

There is a short exercise in Figure 6.6; much has been written about mindfulness so there are a lot of resources available.

Relaxation

While you were engaged in your addictive behavior, it's likely you avoided or didn't make time just for you. Learning to relax may seem like a luxury or an unneeded self-indulgence, but it is beneficial to restoring balance to your life.

Although there are similarities between meditation and relaxation, they aren't the same. Finding ways to relax can be important to your recovery journey. Relaxation is an individual experience so find what works for you. Following are a few relaxation techniques to try:

Progressive Muscle Relaxation

PMR (Figure 6.4) helps you become aware of what your muscles feel like when they're tense and when they're relaxed. In this exercise, you'll tense and relax all of your major muscles so when you're done, all of your muscles will be completely relaxed. Many people report feeling immediately refreshed and calmed after doing PMR. You may feel this, or you may feel nothing, especially in the beginning.

You can do PMR lying down or in a chair. Tense each muscle group, hold for five seconds, then relax. This helps you feel each muscle group in a tense state and then in a relaxed one.

Here is an example of how to tense and relax each major muscle group:

Figure 6.4. **PMR exercises.**

Body area	Exercises
Head	Wrinkle your forehead Close your eyes tightly Open your mouth wide Push your tongue against the roof of your open mouth Clench your jaw tightly
Neck and shoulders	Shrug your shoulders toward your ears Press your shoulder blades together
Arms and hands	Clench your hands into fists Curl your biceps in toward your chest Extend your arms straight and push against an invisible wall
Stomach, lower back, hips, buttocks	Tighten your stomach muscles Arch your back Tighten your hip and butt muscles
Thighs, calves, ankles, feet, toes	Push your thighs together Tense your calf muscles Flex your ankles, bringing your feet toward your body Curl your toes under Bring your to back toward your body

Visualization

Our imagination is more powerful than we realize. In addition to using visualization as a way to relax, you can use it to prepare for job interviews, difficult conversations, and even for goals you want to achieve. Athletes use visualization to enhance performance. Figure skaters spend focused time visualizing their entire routines. Public speakers often visualize going through their presentations before giving them.

For this relaxation exercise, allow yourself about 15 minutes. Make sure you don't feel rushed and that distractions are at a minimum. Sit or lie down in a comfortable, quiet place.

Figure 6.5. **Visualization exercise.**

Close your eyes and see yourself entering into a quiet, safe, and relaxing place alone.
Fill your place with details of what you hear and smell, what you are sitting or lying on.
Create in your mind the noises and smells that you find relaxing.
Fill this place with as much detail as you can about things that relax you.
Let your body relax and your shoulders and head fall gently.
Breathe slowly.

Meditation

Meditation and mindfulness are not usually part of a SMART meeting; however, some people set aside some time each day for mindfulness meditation.

Figure 6.6. **Meditation guide.**

Sit in a comfortable upright posture, with a straight but not rigid back. Try not to slouch as this affects your breathing, and breathing is an important part of meditation.

Breathe slowly through your nose. Fill your lungs. Notice how your diaphragm expands and your tummy sticks out when you breathe in. Put your hands on your stomach just below the belly button to feel this sensation.

Close your eyes. Take three deep, long breaths, noticing how it feels.

Now, let your breath settle to a normal rhythm. On the out-breath, silently count "one." On the next out-breath, count "two," and so on up to 10. When you get to 10, go back to one. If you lose count, just start again at one.

Feel the physical sensation of your breathing. Thoughts will enter your mind. Don't try to push them away or pretend they don't exist. Simply recognize their presence but don't engage them. If you find your mind wandering, gently turn your attention back to your breathing and counting. Don't judge yourself or your meditation "abilities."

Do this for the time you decided in advance and try not to give up early. Set a timer so you don't have to check a clock.

This exercise helps you learn to be "in the moment" and let emotional upset subside without reacting in an unhelpful way.

Meditation takes practice. At first, you may only be able to meditate for a few minutes, but the more you do it, the longer you'll be able to do it. You'll meditate better some days than others. That's normal. It helps if you do it the same time and same place every day.

Some people sit on pillows in the Buddhist lotus position with their hands resting on their knees, palms upward. Others sit in a comfortable chair. You may want to burn a candle or incense. Meditative music may help, too. Experiment to find what works best for you.

You also can practice being mindful wherever you are, noticing what you feel and think, the taste of your food, the presence of other; just being aware of the world around and within you.

Pay attention to the present and those excessive emotions, and ruminating and troublesome thoughts may begin to trouble you less.

Regaining your health

Nutrition

After you stop an addictive behavior, you may find that your appetite returns. Healthy eating and maintaining a balanced diet are essential to good living. Going out for an occasional meal with friends or family can be fun. Making a shopping list, going to the grocery store, preparing the food, cooking your meals, and cleaning up can be included in your plan for the day. This can help keep you occupied or fill in any spare time you may have.

Even though a person with an addictive behavior may think they are eating normally and regularly, this is generally not the case. Vitamin deficiencies are common, especially with heavy alcohol abuse because water-soluble vitamins — B vitamins, such as thiamine and folic acid, and vitamin C — are washed away frequently because your body doesn't store these nutrients.

It's a good idea to eat meals at regular times to help restore your health. You may consider adding vitamin B and C supplements to your diet. Your doctor may recommend specific vitamin supplements.

Exercise

Any form of physical exercise is beneficial. If you can't join a gym or don't have the stamina to lift weights or do brisk aerobics, then take walks or ride a bike. Exercise doesn't have to be strenuous to be beneficial. A 30-minute walk five days a week can be enjoyable and is known to reverse the effects of depression. Build up gradually if you have not exercised for a while.

Physical activity can help relieve tension and refresh you. You'll get the most benefit if you can exercise for at least 30 minutes three days a week. Make sure it is not too strenuous if you have not exercised for a while. Periodic breaks such as a brisk walk or going for a swim can rejuvenate the body and make you feel more positive and productive.

You may want to check with your doctor before starting an exercise routine to make sure you're healthy enough for even mild exercise.

Sleep

Sleep patterns can change when a person stops drinking or using drugs. This is normal; your body needs time to adjust. If you have difficulty sleeping, cutting down on caffeine will help. Taking a short walk in the evening or reading a book in bed also may help.

It may take weeks to recover from sleep deficit and to start sleeping normally. Vivid, sometimes disturbing dreams are common early in recovery. Sleep patterns usually improve.

Medication

SMART Recovery supports the scientifically informed use of psychological treatment and legally prescribed psychiatric and addiction medication.

If you have depression, anxiety, or other nonaddictive disorders, feel free to pursue treatment and medications. SMART will support you if you choose to use medications designed to help with substance dependence and smoking cessation.

Procrastination

We all procrastinate to some degree; however, problematic procrastination can resemble addictive behavior and become a detrimental habit. You can apply what you have learned about overcoming addictive behavior to overcoming procrastination.

Procrastination is too complex to address here, but here are a few points to keep in mind:

- Procrastination is a universal — and sometimes even useful — human behavior.
- It can be a form of self-sabotage.
- Like anything, if it's extreme, it's potentially harmful.
- It can be associated with trying to avoid strong emotions such as anxiety.
- It may be a signal that you have lingering ambivalence about recovery.
- Procrastination can weaken your ability to achieve your goals.
- It can be addressed with a CBA.

Summary

Living a balanced life is scary, exhilarating, and authentic. Experiment with different aspects of your life to determine what adds value and balance. This is your life and you get to choose how to live it.

Setting goals, planning tasks, and developing a VACI are important building blocks to your new life.

SMART will continue to help you maintain your change and your self-empowerment. Continue using the tools that help you and attend meetings whenever you want. The skills that you acquired along your recovery journey will prove invaluable to you when facing future situations.

Always remember that you have the power to create your life.

Chapter 7: **SMART Science**

In our pursuit to provide the best possible science and recovery techniques, we adjust and update the SMART program as new insights and learning emerge from research. Millions of dollars are spent every year to understand the nature of addiction and how to recover from it. There are gaps in what is known but vastly more is understood today than a couple of decades ago.

We work as a partner with people in recovery and with professionals, including psychologists and researchers interested in addiction. This partnership benefits all involved by tracking developments in the science — what research suggests will work. Plus, our large team of trained facilitators provide feedback on what seems to be practical and effective in our meetings. We also have an International Advisory Council with some of the most well-respected researchers in addiction and mental health from whom we can seek advice.

As with any mutual-help program, there is little research on the effectiveness of SMART Recovery as a whole; however, the individual tools and methods are supported by enough evidence to conclude that they are effective. There also is solid research supporting the vital role that mutual-help groups play in a person's recovery.

How we use science

One of the aspects of addiction is that there is no single model that provides a "universal theory" about the phenomenon of addiction. Instead, science offers a broad set of overlapping, competing, and evolving set of theories and models. These include biochemical explanations of how addiction works in the brain, psychological explanations of how addiction is structured into the way we think, and how addiction and recovery need to be understood in the context of social relationships. The scientific consensus is that these three aspects each play a part in addiction. It's called the "bio-psycho-social" model.

In practice, the tools and methods of SMART are taken mostly from psychological understandings of addiction and behavior change. It's helpful to have a basic understanding of the brain chemistry of addiction. Our tools and methods are consistent with current neuroscience research. SMART Recovery supports the scientifically informed use of legally prescribed psychiatric and addiction medication, as well as psychological treatments.

Recovery is a complex and individual process. What helps one person may not help another. What helps during the early days of recovery may not be what is important several years later. SMART offers a rounded program of recovery. We try to help participants at all stages, from their first meeting when they might not have begun a serious attempt at change, to those who have been abstaining for years.

This breadth of interest leads us to draw from many theoretical models, methods, and ideas. Not all of the ideas or tools within these approaches are relevant to SMART Recovery. We look for tools that are practical within our mutual-help model:

- Cognitive Behavior Therapy

- Rational Emotive Behavior Therapy

- Motivational Interviewing

- Transtheoretical Model of Behavior Change

- Recovery Communities and Mutual Aid

- Recovery Capital

- Therapeutic Lifestyle Change

- Third-wave CBT including Dialectical Behavior Therapy (DBT) and Acceptance and Commitment Therapy (ACT)

No approach to recovery will work for everyone; we know we don't have all the answers. Some participants use only SMART Recovery meetings (perhaps supplemented by online activities and our publications). Others combine SMART meetings with attendance at other meetings, such as 12-step groups, or work with a mental health professional.

For more about the science of addiction recovery, visit:

www.drugabuse.gov/publications, Principles of Drug Addiction Treatment by NIDA

www.behaviortherapy.com/whatworks, what works in alcohol treatment, as listed in the *Handbook of Alcoholism Treatment*

nrepp.samhsa.gov, The National Registry of Evidence-based Programs and Practices

DSM-V

The fourth edition of the American Psychiatric Association's (APA) Diagnostic and Statistical Manual of Mental Disorders (DSM IV-TR) used by medical professionals to diagnose clinical mental health conditions was updated in May 2013.

The DSM-V added a new and separate section of "behavioral addictions" containing the single disorder that covers compulsive gambling. This allows other types of behavioral compulsions not covered elsewhere in the DSM-V to be recognized as addictive behaviors if they meet the same diagnostic criteria as gambling.

The DSM-V defines different types of addictive or compulsive behavior comprehensively and recognizes that these terms may apply to other types of behavioral disorders beyond those that involve alcohol or drug use.

Chapter 8: **SMART Tools and Strategies Matrix**

In chapters 3 through 6, we presented several tools that can help you through recovery. Appendix B includes blank templates of each of tools. Make copies of them to use often.

Below is a matrix that maps the SMART tools to the Stages of Change to help you identify what tools are most helpful at each stage.

Table 8.1. **Matrix: Stages of Change, strategies, tools.**

Stage of Change	Strategies	SMART Tools
Precontemplation: "I don't have a problem. Don't bug me. I'm just 'visiting' this meeting."	Try to see your whole situation Attend SMART meetings Explore SMART website Drinker's Checkup	Hierarchy of Values (HOV)
Contemplation: "I want to change (I think)." Ambivalent rather than unmotivated or in denial.	Clarify your situation	HOV Cost-Benefit Analysis (CBA) Change Plan worksheet
Preparation: "I know I need to change, but how do I do it?"	Consider your options Take small steps Look ahead, not backward	CBA Update Change Plan Manage urges using DISARM, basic strategies
Action: "Now, I'm working on changing my addictive behaviors."	Gain an understanding of your addictive behaviors Build relationships Identify and commit to trying new coping strategies	ABC Update Change Plan Identify SMART strategies to manage urges
Maintenance: "I'm committed to and sticking with abstinence."	Enjoy confidence you're building Be wary of temptations Learning to plan Review relapse prevention	ABC Lifestyle Balance Pie HOV VACI worksheet to review interests and activities
Exit: "Moving on to the rest of my life."	You've adopted a new normal and self-image Attend SMART meetings when you want to or need to	CBA Lifestyle Balance Pie ABC

Chapter 9: **Family & Friends**

While most of the Handbook is for people who suffer from addictive behaviors, this chapter is for their family and friends, also known as concerned significant others (CSO). We use those terms interchangeably.

A person with an addictive behavior isn't the only one affected by it. Their CSOs are affected, too. Deeply.

If you're in a relationship with someone who suffers from addictive behavior, it's a difficult journey; SMART Recovery can help you, too.

CRAFT

SMART uses a science-based program called Community Reinforcement Approach and Family Training (CRAFT) that recommends new ways to interact with your loved one that enhance your ability to influence positive change.

CRAFT's approach proved twice as likely as the Johnson intervention and six times as likely as Al-Anon to get a loved one into treatment. CRAFT is based on proven behavioral principles and CBT techniques. It teaches positive, nonconfrontational strategies such as rewarding positive behaviors instead of engaging in emotionally charged confrontations that may actually push a loved one to use or act out.

CRAFT has three major goals:

1. Improve the quality of your life, regardless of your loved one's choices.

2. Influence your loved one to reduce their using.

3. Influence your loved one to pursue recovery.

It also can help you learn how to deal with your loved one compassionately rather than with hostility, frustration, or avoidance.

An excellent book called *Get Your Loved One Sober: Alternatives to Nagging, Pleading, and Threatening* by Robert J. Meyers, Ph.D., and Brenda L. Wolfe, Ph.D., explains CRAFT and is the mainstay of SMART's Family & Friends program. The book provides tools and scenarios to help you learn how to use CRAFT.

Using plain language and real examples, the book teaches you how to:

- Stop fixing your loved one's messes.

- Take control of your life and your relationship.

- Map new behavioral patterns.

- Recognize when a situation becomes dangerous.

- Create a rapid exit plan.

- Encourage your loved one into professional treatment.
- Identify your loved one's triggers for using or acting out.
- Support your loved one's recovery.
- Use new techniques to solve old problems.

Online meeting and forum

SMART offers a Family & Friends meeting online and there are some face-to-face meetings, too. Check our website regularly for news about new face-to-face meetings.

Meeting topics range from self-care to problem solving, and may focus on an issue, such as establishing boundaries, communicating in nonconfrontational ways, or setting goals.

There also is an online Message Board forum for F&F on SMART Recovery Online (SROL). In this forum, you can share your thoughts, ideas, questions, and concerns. F&F participants offer support and share experiences with each other in a safe and supportive environment. Others in the SMART community frequently join the discussions and share their perspectives as well.

Publications

The SMART Recovery Family & Friends Handbook is a terrific resource for people affected by the addictive behavior of a loved one.

And, trained SMART facilitators interested in starting a Family & Friends meeting in their community will benefit from the Family & Friends Facilitator's Manual, which is a guide to conducting Family & Friends meetings.

Chapter 10: **About SMART**

Purpose, Mission, and Vision

- **Purpose**: To help individuals gain independence from addictive behavior and lead meaningful and satisfying lives. To support the availability of choices in recovery.

- **Mission**: To offer no-fee, self-empowering, science-based, face-to-face, and online support groups for abstaining from any substance or activity addictive behavior.

- **Vision**: Think SMART Worldwide.

From these statements, it's easy to see what SMART is about and where it wants to go. SMART is a network of volunteers with only a small administrative staff. We are a global organization offering experience, knowledge, and support to people suffering from any type of addictive behavior.

History

SMART Recovery began as the Rational Recovery Self-Help Network. In 1994 we ended our affiliation with RR and changed our name to SMART Recovery. Since then have focused on building a network of volunteers around the world and in creating a website to offer online services to those who can't, or don't want to, attend face-to-face meetings. Today, hundreds of face-to-face meetings are held all over the world, and more are added every year.

SMART volunteers and support

We rely primarily on volunteers to move the organization forward; they are supported by a small staff. Volunteers include:

- Board of Directors

- International Advisory Council

- Regional Coordinators

- Committee Members

- Advisors

- Facilitators

- Online message board, meeting, and chat room volunteers

Many of our volunteers have gone through recovery and find that reaching out to others helps them maintain their commitment to a healthier life.

If you're just beginning your recovery, you have hard work ahead of you. In the early stages, that's enough to focus on. Eventually, you may want to volunteer with SMART to help others.

We are a growing organization and can use help in promoting SMART as a recovery option. Even if you don't have the time or interest to volunteer, you can still support us in other ways:

- Mention SMART in conversations as a free addictive behavior recovery program.

- Hand out SMART brochures in your community and to those who might need help.

- Let local health professionals, clergy, law enforcement, and legal professionals know about SMART.

- Donate SMART books and materials to local libraries.

- Subscribe to the free quarterly *News & Views* newsletter, available online.

- Share your story by submitting articles for the newsletter.

- Tell local media, human services departments, charities, intervention, and treatment centers about SMART.

- Be an advocate — tell others about SMART if you think they, or someone they know, could benefit from our approach and support.

Donations

SMART Recovery relies on the generosity of individuals to help sustain our programs and services. In addition to personal donations, money comes in from publication sales, meeting groups that share their collections with the Central Office, and training fees and website supporters.

All donations are welcome and are tax-deductible in the U.S. You may visit our website and click on the donate button, or send a check, money order or credit card information to:

SMART Recovery Central Office
7304 Mentor Ave., Suite F
Mentor, OH 44060

Policies

While we want to keep SMART as simple as possible, giving each person the latitude to work their own recovery, we have developed some policies and positions on certain topics.

Medication

SMART Recovery supports the scientifically informed use of psychological treatment and legally prescribed psychiatric and addiction medication.

Disease model

SMART Recovery tools can help you regardless of whether or not you believe addiction is a disease.

Confidentiality

Recovery is a personal journey. In face-to-face meetings and on SROL, people openly discuss their lives. We want everyone to feel safe in these meetings, knowing that their privacy will be protected. Do not tell anyone outside of a meeting any information or details that could identify an individual. If you see someone outside of a meeting, do not identify them as meeting attendees. If you violate confidentiality, you may be barred from SMART meetings.

Personal responsibility

Drinking alcohol, taking drugs, or engaging in potentially harmful activities are matters of personal choice. You're welcome at meetings whether or not you are currently using. If your behavior disrupts the meeting, you may be asked to leave. However, our policy is not to shame you or pressure you into stopping your addictive behavior.

Respect

Show respect for others at all times. Don't label anyone, or use offensive or denigrating language or behavior in meetings or on SROL. Threats, intimidation, violence, and other nonrespectful behaviors is not tolerated in meetings or online.

Spirituality

We believe that the power to change addictive behaviors resides within each individual and does not depend upon adherence to any spiritual viewpoint. The use of religious or spiritual beliefs and practices in recovery is a personal choice and not a part of our program.

Appendix A: **Definitions of Terms**

Term	Definition
4-Point Program®	A registered trademark of SMART Recovery. The program addresses four elements that help people recover from addictive behavior: 1. Building and maintaining motivation 2. Coping with urges 3. Managing thoughts, feelings, and emotions 4. Living a balanced life
ABC	An acronym from the first three components of a Rational Emotive Behavioral Therapy tool to help change thinking, attitude, and beliefs about events and emotions. It contains these components: **A**ctivating event **B**elief (irrational) about the event **C**onsequences of irrational belief **D**isputing irrational belief and replacing it with a new one **E**ffective new belief
Acting out	Acting on an impulse or craving without first thinking about it.
Activating event	See ABC. Also known as a trigger, any action, thought, sight, smell, emotion, or other stimuli that we associate with our addictive behavior.
ADASHN, Inc.	Alcohol and Drug Abuse Self-Help Network, Inc. is the registered legal name of SMART Recovery. ADASHN does business as SMART Recovery.
Addictive behavior	Any activity, substance, object, or behavior that has become the major focus of a person's life to the exclusion of other activities, or that has begun to harm the individual or others physically, mentally, or emotionally.
Cost-Benefit Analysis (**CBA**)	A SMART tool to help you identify the long- and short-term advantages and disadvantages of an addictive behavior, decision, etc.
Cognitive Behavioral Therapy (**CBT**)	An approach that addresses excessive emotions, thoughts, and unhelpful behaviors by using goal-oriented, specific systems. Many of SMART's tools are based on CBT. REBT is one version of CBT.
Coping	Refers to our ability to deal with stress and urges to use.
Disputing Irrational Beliefs (**DIBs**)	A technique to look at the underlying beliefs or assumptions we hold about something.
Destructive Images Self-talk Awareness and Refusal Method (**DISARM**)	A reminder to consider the accuracy and helpfulness of our thoughts, and to refuse to let them guide our behavior if they are inaccurate or unhelpful.

Rational Emotive Behavior Therapy (**REBT**)	Developed in the 1950s by Dr. Albert Ellis, it is based on the principle that most of our problems originate with how we interpret events in the world rather than the actual effects of those events on our lives.
Stages of Change	A model explaining change as a process, first developed by Prochaska and DiClemente in the 1970s.
Trigger	See activating event. Anything — a smell, image, event, sound, time of day, etc. — that a person connects with acting out. This doesn't mean that a trigger automatically leads to acting out; however, many of our thoughts and emotions may be connected to these triggers, especially in the early stages of recovery. Also called a cue.
Urge	A strong desire to use or act out.
Using	Common term in drug or alcohol addictive behavior but can apply to any compulsive behavior. We "use" when we engage in compulsive shopping or gambling to escape our problems.
Vital Absorbing Creative Interest (**VACI**)	A a productive and fulfilling endeavor to pursue that is meaningful and that replaces time previously spent on your addictive behavior.

Appendix B: **Worksheets**

Figure 3.1. **Hierarchy of Values.**

What I value most
1.
2.
3.
4.
5.

Figure 3.3. **Change-Plan worksheet.**

Changes I want to make:	
How important is it to me to make these changes? (1-10 scale)	
How confident am I that I can make these changes? (1-10 scale)	
The most important reasons I want to make these changes are:	
The steps I plan to take in changing are:	

How other people can help me:	
Person	Kind of help

I will know my plan is working when:

Some things that could interfere with my plan are:

Figure 3.4. **Cost-Benefit Analysis.**

Using or Doing	
Label each item short-term (ST) or long-term (LT)	
Benefits (rewards and advantages)	**Costs** (risks and disadvantages)

NOT Using or Doing	
Label each item short-term (ST) or long-term (LT)	
Benefits (rewards and advantages)	**Costs** (risks and disadvantages)

Figure 4.4. **Urge Log.**

Date	Time	Rate 1-10	Length of urge	What triggered my urge?	Where/who was I with?	How I coped and my feelings about coping	Alternative activities, substitute behaviors

Figure 4.6. **Weekly Planner.**

Time	Monday	Tuesday	Wednesday	Thursday	Friday	Saturday	Sunday
Morning							
Midday							
Evening							

Figure 4.9 & 5.5. **ABC.**

Activating event	**B**elief about event — irrational	**C**onsequence of my irrational belief	**D**ispute my irrational belief	**E**ffective change in my thinking

Figure 5.1. **Disputing Irrational Beliefs (DIBs).**

My irrational belief	Question my IB	My rational belief

Figure 6.1. **Lifestyle Balance Pie.**

Date _____

This exercise and graphic is based on the work of Julia Cameron's *The Artist's Way*, and is used by permission from Penguin Publishers.

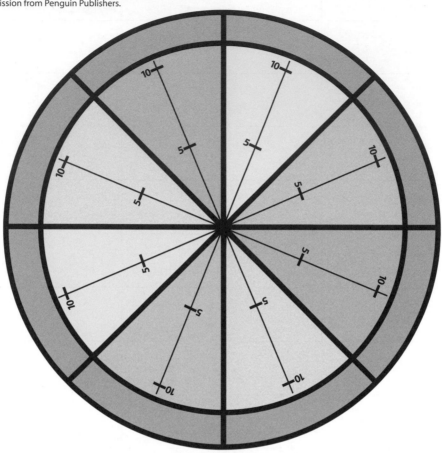

Lowest scores	
Life category	**Score**
1.	
2.	
3.	
4.	
Highest scores	
4.	
3.	
2.	
1.	
Plan	

Figure 6.3. **Goal setting.**

Life category (from Lifestyle Balance Pie):				
Related to value (from HOV):				
Goal:				
Specific	**M**easurable	**A**greeable	**R**ealistic	**T**ime-bound
Revised goal (if needed):				
Specific	**M**easurable	**A**greeable	**R**ealistic	**T**ime-bound
Tasks/objects to reach goal:				

Life category (from Lifestyle Balance Pie):				
Related to value (from HOV):				
Goal:				
Specific	**M**easurable	**A**greeable	**R**ealistic	**T**ime-bound
Revised goal (if needed):				
Specific	**M**easurable	**A**greeable	**R**ealistic	**T**ime-bound
Tasks/objects to reach goal:				

Appendix C: **Recommended Reading and Resources**

SMART's publications (Available at SMART's online bookstore)

SMART Recovery Handbook — A compilation of practical information designed to assist the reader in attaining the ultimate goal of recovery.

SMART Recovery Family & Friends Handbook — Designed for people affected by the addictive behavior of a loved one, this 138 page Handbook contains 14 sections with a wide range of topics including: Change and Motivation, Positive Communication, Healthy Boundaries, Safety and Support, Coping with Lapses, Disable the Enabling, Trust and Forgiveness – and much more. It can be used in conjunction with attendance at SMART Family & Friends (F&F) online or community meetings, or on its own.

SMART Recovery Teen Handbook — Developed with a grant from The Community Coalition for Teens in Greenfield, Massachusetts.

SMART Recovery Facilitator's Manual — This how-to manual provides an excellent overview of how to start a SMART Recovery group meeting, and also serves as a superb refresher for individuals who have been leading groups for some time.

SMART Recovery Family & Friends Facilitator's Manual — This how-to Manual provides information for conducting a SMART Recovery Family & Friends Meeting using a combination of SMART's tools and CRAFT (Community Reinforcement and Family Training) concepts. It explores: Change and Motivation, Positive Communication, Healthy Boundaries, Safety and Support, Coping with Lapses, Disable the Enabling, Trust and Forgiveness – and much more. The Manual is used in conjunction with SMART's FAST Distance Training.

Addiction and Co-Occurring Disorders from a SMART Recovery Perspective: A Manual for Group Therapists — by Dawn Adamson, RN, CPMHN(c), CARN, and A.G. Ahmed, MD, FRCP, This manual aims to engage the individual in the recovery process, increase individual insight, motivate and sustain change through education and skill development. The program has been adapted and delivered in a community setting to individuals with co-occurring mental disorders.

SMART Recovery Motivational Guide and Workbook for Recovering Healthcare Professionals — by Maria Elsa Rodriguez, DNP, ACNS-BC, Chapter topics include: Motivation; The Prevalence of Addiction in Healthcare Providers (physicians, nurses, psychologists, pharmacists and dentists); Information About SMART Recovery; The Brain, Drugs, & Motivation; An Overview of Cognitive-Behavioral Therapy; The Transtheoretical Model of Change; Self-Efficacy; Self-Esteem and Self-Worth; Locus of Control; Resilience; Coping Skills for Emotions & Behaviors; and an Appendix reviewing The Background and History of Narcotic & Alcohol Use in the United States. A number of interactive activities are included throughout the workbook.

Addictive Behavior

For SMART participants or family and friends:

Alcohol: How to Give it Up and Be Glad You Did, A Sensible Approach — Philip Tate, Ph.D. (See Sharp Press 1997)

Sex, Drugs, Gambling, & Chocolate: A Workbook for Overcoming Addictions — Thomas Horvath, Ph.D. (Impact Publishers, Inc. - 1998)

The Small Book — Jack Trimpey, LCSW (Delacorte Press, New York, NY - 1992)

When AA Doesn't Work for You: Rational Steps to Quitting Alcohol - Albert Ellis, Ph.D. and Emmett Velten, Ph.D. (Barricade Books, Inc., Fort Lee, NJ - 1992)

Recovery Options: The Complete Guide — Volpicelli & Szalavitz (John Wiley & Sons, Inc. 2000-2002)

Resisting 12-Step Coercion — Stanton Peele, Charles Bufe, and Archie Brodsky (See Sharp Press - 2000)

Sober for Good: New Solutions for Drinking Problems — Advice from those who have Succeeded – Anne Fletcher (Houghton Mifflin Co. 2001)

The Truth About Addiction and Recovery — Stanton Peele, Ph.D. and Archy Brodsky with Mary Arnold (Simon & Schuster - 1989)

Get Your Loved One Sober: Alternatives to Nagging, Pleading, and Threatening — Robert J. Meyers, Ph.D., and Brenda L. Wolfe, Ph.D. (Hazelden Publishing and Educational Services 2004)

The Authoritative Guide to Self Help Books — Santrock, Minnett, and Campbell (Guilford Press - 1994)

Changing for Good — James Prochaska, Ph.D., John Norcross, Ph.D. and Carlo DiClemente, Ph.D. (Wm. Morrow & Company, New York, NY - 1994)

For facilitators and volunteer advisors

The Handbook of Alcoholism Treatment Approaches: Effective Alternatives (3rd edition) — Hester and Milller, eds. (Allyn & Bacon 2003)

Managing Addictions: Cognitive, Emotive and Behavioral Techniques — F. M. Bishop, Ph.D. (Albert Ellis Institute 2001)

Motivational Interviewing (2nd ed.) — Miller and Rollnick (Guilford Publications, Inc. April 2002)

Principles of Drug Addiction Treatment: A Research Based Guide — National Institute on Drug Abuse, www.drugabuse.gov

Websites

www.smartrecovery.org

www.health.org

For facilitators and volunteer advisors

www.abct.org

www.mindtools.com

General behavior change

Manuals to guide change

Coping Better...Anytime, Anywhere — Maxie Maultsby (Rational Self-Help Aids 1990)

Feeling Good — David Burns (Signet, 1980)

How to Stubbornly Refuse to Make Yourself Miserable About Anything, Yes Anything! — Albert Ellis, Ph.D. (Lyle Stuart, Inc., Secaucus, NJ - 1988)

Three Minute Therapy, Change Your Thinking, Change your Life — Michael Edelstein, Ph.D. (Glenbridge Publishing, Ltd. - 1998)

When I Say No I Feel Guilty — Manuel Smith (Bantam/Nonfiction Re-issue Edition Feb. 1, 1975)

Other resources

DVDs (For an updated list of SMART Recovery DVDs, visit our online bookstore)

Facilitating a Basic SMART Recovery Meeting — To attract and train new facilitators. An important tool for anyone who wants to become a trained SMART facilitator.

Facilitating an Advanced SMART Recovery Meeting — Features Jonathan von Breton and Emmett Velten's training program that reviews our program tools. This video presentation helps meeting facilitators address some of the more significant issues that may arise during SMART meetings.

The SMART 4-Point Program® — Features Dr. Joseph Gerstein and Dr. Michler Bishop. They review each point, their underlying principles, and the tools and techniques associated with the points.

SMART Recovery: Who We Are — An overview of SMART; a great tool to acquaint people with program concepts.

SMART Recovery Addiction Recovery in the 21st Century — Joseph Gerstein, M.D., presenting SMART Recovery to addiction professionals at the Maine Medical Center, in which he makes clear the importance of choice of treatment and choice of mutual-help groups is needed. He explains why some are more successful in overcoming substance abuse if they are offered the option of a rational, cognitive approach.

Podcasts

Our list of podcasts is ever growing, and represents a wide array of guest speakers on topics of interest to our participants and volunteers. Topics such as procrastination, *The Art of Living* series, *Combating Depression, Preventing and Coping with Relapse* ... and much more. Visit smartrecovery.libsyn.com for the full library.